HOWARD BRENTON

BERLIN BERTIE

A Royal Court Programme/Text published by

NICK HERN BOOKS
London

A Nick Hern Book

Berlin Bertie first published in 1992 as an original paperback by
Nick Hern Books, a Random Century Company, 20 Vauxhall
Bridge Road, London SW1V 2SA

Berlin Bertie copyright © 1992 by Howard Brenton

Front cover from a design by Lolli Aboutboul

Set in Baskerville by SX Composing, Rayleigh, Essex
Printed by Cox and Wyman Ltd, Reading, Berks

A CIP catalogue record for this book is available from the British
Library

ISBN 1-85459-153-3

The Royal Court Theatre presents

Berlin Bertie

by Howard Brenton

First performance at the Royal Court Theatre:

9 April 1992

Part of a season supported by Wilde Sapte, Solicitors

Recipient of an Arts Council Incentive Funding Award

Financially assisted by the

London Borough of Kensington and Chelsea

The history of the English Stage Company

The history of the English Stage Company is generally held to have begun with the production of John Osborne's **Look Back in Anger** in May 1956. Since then, the Royal Court has consistently been seen as the flagship of new writing.

First and foremost the aim of the English Stage Company is to develop and produce the best in new writing for the theatre, encouraging playwrights from all sections of society to address the problems and possibilities of our times. Early Court writers included John Osborne, Arnold Wesker, John Arden, David Storey, Ann Jellicoe, N F Simpson and Edward Bond. They were followed by a generation of writers led by David Hare and Howard Brenton and, in more recent years, celebrated house writers have included Caryl Churchill, Timberlake Wertenbaker, Robert Holman and Jim Cartwright. Many of their plays are now

regarded as modern classics. The Royal Court has also enjoyed great box office success, most recently with such plays as **Serious Money, Our Country's Good, My Mother Said I Never Should, A Whistle in the Dark** and **Three Birds Alighting on a Field.**

In line with the policy of nurturing new writing, the Theatre Upstairs has mainly been seen as a place for exploration and experiment, where writers can hone their craft prior to the demands of the Mainstage auditorium. In 1991, Winsome Pinnock's **Talking in Tongues** met with both critical and popular acclaim. She has now been commissioned for the Main House. Other graduates to have moved from Upstairs to Down are Anne Devlin, Andrea Dunbar, Sarah Daniels, Jim Cartwright and Clare McIntyre. Most recently, the Theatre Upstairs has proved its value as a focal point for the new work with

the production of Chilean writer Ariel Dorfman's **Death and the Maiden**. This was originally staged as part of LIFT '91 and now, after a sell-out run in the Main House, has moved to the West End. In fact, 1991 saw a record-breaking year at the box office with **Top Girls, Three Birds Alighting on a Field** and **Death and the Maiden** all performing to near capacity.

In the Spring, the Royal Court will host the second **Barclays New Stages Festival**. Last year saw an innovative programme which included Rose English, Graeme Miller, Adventures in Motion Pictures and Dogs in Honey.

Last November, Max Stafford-Clark was re-appointed as Artistic Director and Stephen Daldry was appointed as Artistic Director Designate from 1 April 1992. He will take over as Artistic Director in October 1993. This double appointment was largely greeted with disapproval by the press. We remain quietly optimistic.

The Recruiting Officer photo John Haynes
top **Three Sisters** photo Tom Lawlor

Berlin Bertie

by **Howard Brenton**

cast in order of appearance

Sandy	**Kevin Allen**
Alice	**Penny Downie**
Joanne	**Susan Lynch**
Berlin Bertie	**Nicholas Woodeson**
Rosa	**Diana Rigg**

There will be one interval

The play is set in South London.
The action takes place over the
three days of Easter, 1990.

Director **Danny Boyle**

Designer **Paul McCauley**

Lighting **Rory Dempster**

Sound **Bryan Bowen**

Costume Supervisor **Jennifer Cook**

Assistant Director **Danny Carrick**

Stage Manager **Gemma Bodley**

DSM **Justine Gallacio**

ASM **Michelle Jackson**

Student ASM **Clare Grainger**

Fight Director **Terry King**

Mime Adviser **Chris Widdicombe**

Poster Design **Lolli Aboutboul**

Production Photographer **John Haynes**

Leaflet Design **Sightlines**

The Royal Court would like to thank the following for their generous support of this production

Wardrobe by Persil and Comfort; Ioniser for the control room by The London Ioniser Centre; cordless drill by Makita Electric (UK) Ltd; watches by The Timex Corporation; refrigerators by Electrolux and Phillips Major Appliances Ltd; kettles for rehearsals by Morphy Richards; video for casting purposes by Hitachi; back stage coffee machine by Cona; furniture by Knoll International; freezer for backstage use supplied by Zanussi Ltd 'Now that's a good idea'. Thanks to Casio for use of DAT equipment; closed circuit TV cameras and monitors by Mitsubishi UK Ltd. Natural Spring Water by Wye Spring Water, 149 Cline Square, London SW1. tel 071 730 6977. Overhead projector from WH Smith.

Howard Brenton

For the Royal Court: Revenge; Christie in Love; Fruit; Magnificence; Sore Throats; The Genius; Sleeping Policemen; Bloody Poetry; Greenland; Iranian Nights (with Tariq Ali). Other theatre includes: Brassneck (with David Hare); Epsom Downs; The Romans in Britain; Thirteenth Night; Weapons of Happiness; Pravda (with David Hare); The Churchill Play; Hess is Dead; Moscow Gold (with Tariq Ali).
Adaptations include: Galileo; Danton's Death.
TV includes: Brassneck, The Saliva Milkshake, Desert of Lies, Dead Head (four episodes) (BBC); The Paradise Run (Thames). Novel: Diving for Pearls.

Kevin Allen

Theatre includes: Silly Cow (Haymarket); The Unseen Hand (Bridge Lane); A Prayer for Wings (Bush Theatre & Edinburgh Festival).
TV includes: Murder Most Horrid, Jealousy, GLC and numerous episodes of Comic Strip; The Trials of OZ, Colin's Sandwich, The Firm, He's Asking for It; French & Saunders (BBC); Press Gang, The Bullshitters (Channel Four); A Great Day For Making Friends (WTV).

Films include: A Shocking Accident; The Man Who Shot Xmas; Laughter House; GettingBye; Eat the Rich; Lovechild; Never Come Morning. Directed: Glenn Hoddle, Glen Maderios (Old Red Lion); Video Diaries – On the March with Bobbies Army (World Cup Football – 1990); Booze, Bores, Barbours and Brilliance (Rugby World Cup 1991) (BBC2); Loscudetto (S4C).

Danny Boyle

For the Royal Court: Cinders; Salonika; Victory; The Genius; Up to the Sun; Panic; Saved; The Grace of Mary Traverse.
Other theatre includes: The Pretenders; The Last Days of Don Juan; Hess is Dead; The Silent Woman; The Bite of the Night (RSC); Two Planks and a Passion (Greenwich Theatre).
TV includes: Inspector Morse; Masonic Mysteries & Cherubim and Seraphim (Zenith/Central); Arise and Go Now, For the Greater Good, The Hen House, Scout (BBC); Monkeys; The De Lorean Tapes; The Night Watch; Then Venus of Milo Instead. Currently Mr Wroe's Virgins (BBC). As producer: The Rockingham Shoot, Elephant (BBC TV).

Rory Dempster

Many productions at the Royal Court Theatre. Other theatre includes: The Gulf Between US (West Yorkshire Playhouse); The Invisible Man (Theatre Royal, Stratford East); The Cherry Orchard, A Moon for the Misbegotten (Riverside Studios); Weapons of Happiness, Plenty, A Map of the World, The Bay at Nice, Wrecked Eggs, King Lear, The Crucible, Summer, A Month in the Country, Don Juan, After the Fall (Royal National Theatre); All My Sons, Benefactors, The Rocky Horror Show, Sizwe Banzi is Dead, The Island, Comedians, A Life in the Theatre (West End). Opera includes: La Bohème (WNO); Orfeo (ENO); Parsifal (ROH, Covent Garden); The Barber of Seville (Scottish Opera); The Coronation of Poppea (Opera Factory in May).

Penny Downie

Theatre includes: Scenes from a Marriage (Wyndhams Theatre); A Midsummer Night's Dream, Romeo & Juliet, Richard III, Today, The Dream Play, The Castle, Crimes in Hot Countries, A Winter's Tale, Macbeth, The Art of Success, The Plantagenets (RSC). TV includes: EX (Talkback);

Minder (Thames); Campaign (BBC); A Taste for Death (Anglia); Stanley and the Women (Central); Underbelly (BBC). Films include: Cross Talk; Wetherby; Lionheart.

Susan Lynch

Theatre includes: Sixteen Words for Water (Old Red Lion); The Country Wife; Man is Man; The Importance of Being Earnest; Macbeth; They Shoot Horses, Don't They?; Champagne and Roses (Central School of Drama); Romeo and Juliet; The Tempest (Ulster Youth Theatre); Now That's What I Call Gore (UYT at the Royal National Theatre – Lloyds Bank Youth Drama Festival). TV includes: The Bill (Thames). Winner of the first Renaissance Theatre Award (1990).

Paul McCauley

Theatre design includes: The Genius (Lilian Baylis Theatre). Film includes: The Miracle (direction and design). Exhibitions include: Through the Brass Lidded Eye: the first 150 years of Photography (Guinness Group, Dublin). Assistant Designer Opera Theatre, Dublin & Abbey Theatre, Dublin (1987–89). Head of Design at Audio

Visual Centre, University College, Dublin (1989/90).

Diana Rigg

Theatre includes: The Devils; Becket; The Taming of the Shrew; The Art of Seduction (RSC, Aldwych); A Midsummer Night's Dream; Macbeth, The Comedy of Errors; King Lear, Twelfth Night (RSC, Stratford); Abelard and Heloise (Wyndham's & New York); Jumpers, Macbeth, The Misanthrope, Phaedra Brittanica (Royal National Theatre); Pygmalion (Albery Theatre); Night and Day (Phoenix); Heartbreak House (Haymarket); Little Eyolf (Lyric, Hammersmith); Anthony and Cleopatra (Chichester); Wildfire (Phoenix); Follies (Shaftesbury); All for Love (Almeida Theatre); Putting it Together (Old Fire Station, Oxford). TV include: The Avengers; Little Eyolf (BBC); Hedda Gabler (YTV); King Lear (Granada); Bleak House (BBC); Worst Witch (Central) Unexplained Laughter (BBC); Mother Love (BBC). Won 1990 BAFTA Best Actress for Mother Love. Films include: The Hospital; On Her Majesty's Secret Service; Muppet Movie II; A Midsummer Night's Dream, A Little Night Music; Evil Under the Sun; Snow White.

Nicholas Woodeson

For the Royal Court: Doing the Business (May Days Festival). Other Theatre includes: At Our Table (Royal National Theatre); The Homecoming (Comedy Theatre); King John, Sarcophagus, Flight, A Midsummer Night's Dream, Henry V, Red Noses, The Desert Air, The Party, Good (RSC); The Possibilities (Almeida); Man and Superman, Piaf (Broadway); The Art of Success, Strawberry Fields (Manhattan Theatre Club). TV includes: Bonjour La Classe; Maria's Child, A Fatal Inversion; The Wolvis Family; For the Greater Good; Blackeyes; My Kingdom for a Horse; The Hound of the Baskervilles (BBC); The Blackheath Poisonings (Central); Here's Boomer (NBC); A Rumor of War (CBS); Miami Vice. Film includes: Heaven's Gate; Max & Helen; The Russia House.

'Hooks and Eyes and Plays'

I was told the story that, after many transformations, became the plot of Berlin Bertie, while I was visiting East Berlin in February of 1990. It was a brief anecdote. But I knew, even as my informant was speaking, that it was the seed from which a play would grow. I'm afraid that there is a grain of truth in the saying 'Don't tell playwrights

anything personal, it'll come back at you from a stage'. But, in defence of the sometimes unscrupulous behaviour of members of my craft, what we steal from life changes so much that our sources rarely realise they have been robbed.

Back in London, I told the story to Max Stafford-Clark at the Royal Court. He offered a commission, but what I wanted was help. I had the idea of a London episode, set on the coming Easter weekend. Detail

seemed important. I thought that a play about people going through extreme changes should be 'rooted', imagined to have happened on a specific three days. So, with Max's blessing, I got together a monitoring team of people who were working at the Court.

Two years on, I've been looking at the archive we made. Wrapped in bin-liners in my loft are all the newspapers of 13–15 April, 1990; ten video tapes of all channels, and all the ITV, BBC and Sky newscasts; three tape cassettes of radio material; and scrapbook diaries, kept by my helpful monitors, cutting out what caught the eye.

It is odd, and a little disturbing, to see how unreality has begun to tarnish what seemed real only two years ago. What is the odd, false edge of insincerity in the recorded voices? Do accents shift, even in twenty-four months? Mrs Thatcher was meeting President Bush in the Bahamas. In an interview she seems weirdly dated, frivolous, almost camp. It is the Neville Chamberlain effect; when you see some politicians on film and now on video, it seems inconceivable that they ever had power. It has happened very quickly to Mrs Thatcher.

The big news, that Easter, was the 'Iraqi supergun'. Experts appear talking of 'high milling standards', most of them certain that the tubes were not for a gun. Madonna launched her 'cream corset over men's trousers' look at a Tokyo concert. Gorbachev was meeting General Jarawselski of Poland (remember him?). The West Indies were destroying the England Cricket team in the Carribean. The Arsenal manager aquired an American girlfriend - 'Mum leaves baby for soccer boss' (headline of the Sunday Mirror.) Moscow Authorities acknowledged responsibility for the Katyn massacre of Polish partisans. The Sun had a front-page exclusive on Easter Saturday, with a religious theme: 'Naughty Habits of my Nuns'. And Nelson Mandela addressed a packed Wembley Stadium at a concert celebrating his release from prison, two months previously. To the tumultuous, almost all-white audience, who are singing 'you'll never walk alone' ('What is that?' Mandela asks a helper, 'A football song' comes the reply, at which he looks puzzled), he says 'thank you for choosing to care', a remark that will not erode into insincerity.

I finally got to write Berlin Bertie in the summer of 1991. All of the play came to be set in London, not in Berlin. I didn't really use much of the hours of tape and the bale of newsprint we collected (though it did hail on Easter Sunday afternoon in South London, as one of the characters complains). Coleridge described the imagination as a well, into which stories, experiences, half-heard phrases are thrown; they stick to each other, like the hooks and eyes of burrs, and change; then when you draw them up to the light, memories have formed themselves into something else...Mmm. Yes, it is like that.

For I remember how, in February 1990, I caught a tram in East Berlin to keep an appointment in the suburbs; it wandered, rattling along its old rails set in the cobbles, at one time stopping for a lazy ten minutes, for no apparent reason. No one seems to mind. Every one on the tram was very... quiet, sunk in their thoughts, eye-contact an impossibility. The sense of dislocation was overpowering. It was as if the bones had been wrenched from their sockets in that place, but no one was screaming. No one was saying anything at all. Then, at my destination, someone leaned forward over a cup of coffee and said: 'One night in Berlin, last October...'. I was being given the play. I can only hope I've used the gift well.

Howard Brenton

March 1992

Members

The Royal Court Theatre's reputation for high quality and exciting drama attracts world-wide audiences. The way to be most closely associated with Britain's National Theatre of New Writing is to join the Royal Court Theatre Society which provides valuable support for its pioneering work.

Members can take advantage of all these benefits:

● top price tickets (£15) in the main house reduced to £4 on Members' nights; two for every production

● tickets for the Theatre Upstairs (normally £5–£8) reduced to £4 on member's nights; two for every production

● regular members' news-letter giving you advance information about the productions and special ticket offers from other theatres

● priority booking oppor-tunities and inclusion on the Royal Court mailing list

All for £12 per year

Other patronage schemes

Friends

For £40 you will be entitled to one complimentary ticket for every production

For £60 you will be entitled to two complimentary tickets for every production You will receive all the other benefits of the Members.

Associates

For £400 you will be entitled to four complimentary top price tickets for all Main House production and two tickets in the Theatre Upstairs. You will receive all the benefits of the Members and appear in the Main house programmes.

Patrons

For £1000 you can make a personal appearance in our programmes, receive an invitation to the special event of the year and take up to six complimentary top price tickets for four productions. You will receive all the benefits of the members. Corporate entertainment facilities will be available on the evenings you choose to come.

Patrons

Diana Bliss
Michael Hoffman
Celia Imrie
John Mortimer
Timberlake Wertenbaker
Irene Worth

Corporate Patrons

Carlton Communications
Michael Winner Limited
Penguin Books Limited
Peters Fraser and Dunlop
Thames Television plc
The Sunday Times

Associates

Barclays Bank plc
Allan Davis
Henny Gestetner
London Arts Discovery Tours
Nick Hern Books
Greville Poke
Richard Wilson

The Olivier Building Appeal

The Royal Court reached the ripe old age of 100 in September 1988. The theatre was showing its age somewhat, and the centenary was celebrated by the launch of the Olivier Appeal, for £800.000 to repair and improve the building.

Laurence Olivier's long association with the Court - as a schoolboy he first saw Shakespeare here, his first London appearance was here in the 1920's and The Entertainer changed the direction of his career in 1957 – made it natural that he should be the Appeal Patron. After his death Joan Plowright CBE, the Lady Olivier, consented to take over as Patron.

We are now half way to our target. With the generous gifts of our many friends and donors, and an award from the Arts Council's Incentive Fund, we have enlarged and redecorated the bars and front of house areas, installed a new central heating boiler and new air conditioning equipment in both theatres, re-wired many parts of the building, redecorated the dressing rooms and we are gradually upgrading the lighting and sound equipment.

The priorities now are to restore the rather faded Victorian façade of the theatre, replace the ancient roofs and build a rehearsal room on top of the theatre. To do this we need to raise the other half of our original target – £400,000.

Can you help? Every donor is honoured in our programmes and Appeal literature. A tour of the theatre, including its more picturesque parts, can be arranged by ringing Becky Shaw on 071 730 5174. If you would like to help with an event or a gift please ring Graham Cowley, General Manager, on the same number.

"Secure the Theatre's future, and take it forwards towards the new century. For the health of the whole theatrical life of Britain it is essential that this greatly all-providing theatre we love so much and wish so well continues to prosper."
Laurence Olivier (1988)

I would like to donate to The Olivier Building Appeal *(Registered charity number 231242)*

I ENCLOSE A CHEQUE MADE PAYABLE TO
THE OLIVIER BUILDING APPEAL
OR PLEASE DEBIT MY ARTSCARD/ACCESS/VISA/AMEX
ACCOUNT

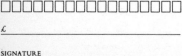

£ _____

SIGNATURE _____

EXPIRY DATE _____

NAME _____

ADDRESS _____

_____

POSTCODE _____

_____

TELEPHONE DAY _____

EVENING _____

Return to The Olivier Building Appeal, Royal Court Theatre, Sloane Square, London, SW1W 8AS

Coming next

Box Office 071 730 1745/2554

main house

18 May – 6 June

Second Barclays
New Stages Festival

Companies performing are:

week one
Brith Gof

week two
**The Cholmondeleys and
The Featherstonehaughs**

week three
Yes/No People
V-TOL

From 11 June
The Royal Court Theatre
in association with
the Theatre of Comedy
present
Six Degrees of Separation
by John Guare

theatre upstairs

now playing
Some Singing Blood
by Heidi Thomas

Chris Ettridge

Julia Ford

Gary McDonald

Anton Rodgers

Prunella Scales

directed by Jules Wright
designed by Fotini Dimou
lighting designed by Stephen Watson

From 30 April
Karate Billy Comes Home
by Klaus Pohl
translated by Lucy Weller
with David Tushingham
directed by Stephen Unwin
designed by Lucy Weller

in the west end
at the Duke of York's Theatre

now booking until 8 August
Death and the Maiden
by Ariel Dorfman

'Best play of 1991' The Times

Death and the Maiden photo Mark Douet
Michael Byrne and Juliet Stevenson

THE NATIONAL ART COLLECTIONS FUND

is Britain's premier art charity

Last year we gave over £2 million to our museums and galleries to help buy works of fine and decorative art. This *Portrait of Anna Aagaard* by Gabriele Münter was acquired by Leicestershire Museum and Art Gallery with the help of a purchase grant from the National Art Collections Fund.

We rely entirely on members' subscriptions, gifts and bequests; we receive no government funding. Members enjoy benefits including The Art Quarterly of the National Art Collections Fund, filled with articles by distinguished writers covering a broad spectrum of the visual arts; a programme of special events nationwide; free entry to art musems; and concessionary rates to many major exhibitions.

Annual membership costs £15; for more details of the benefits of membership, call 071–821 0404 or write to us at 20 John Islip Street, London SW1P 4JX.

BERLIN BERTIE

A play in three acts
by Howard Brenton

Characters

ALICE BRINE

ROSA, ALICE's older sister

SANDY, a boyfriend of ALICE

JOANNE, a girlfriend of ALICE

'BERTOLT BRECHT', a.k.a. 'BERLIN BERTIE'

Ages: ALICE is 31, ROSA is 43, JOANNE is 17, SANDY is 25, 'BERTIE' is 50.

The play is set in South London. Its action takes place over the three days of Easter, 1990.

This text went to press before the opening night on the Main Stage of the Royal Court Theatre and may therefore differ slightly from the play as performed.

ACT ONE

Good Friday, April 13th, 1990.

A ground-floor maisonette flat on a South London housing estate. The flat is a mess. There are piles of discarded newspapers, many of them torn and screwed up. There are unwashed plates and broken crockery amongst them. There is an ironing board that is piled with bottles, cans and the remains of takeaway meals. There are discarded and unwashed clothes. There are lamps on the floor, some without shades and with a mess of wires. It is impossible to walk across the floor without treading on something or having to kick something out of the way. There is a crack diagonally across the window. It has been clumsily repaired with brown sticky tape. There are no curtains. There is a television set. A video machine rests on the top of the television set.

1.

ALICE is lying asleep on the floor. She is swathed in old blankets. Downstage can be seen the feet and calves of a YOUNG WOMAN. It is JOANNE. She lies asleep on her front. Her legs poke out from beneath blankets and newspapers. Her heels are sore. SANDY rails at the sleeping ALICE. He is dressing.

SANDY. Some fucking sense o' responsibility . . . I mean I'm not saying get a grip on your life, not that crap, I'm not saying stop being such a fucking slag, nothing GIANT, I'm not saying be a GOOD PERSON all of a sudden, I'm not saying 'say yes' to changing your life inside out when the fucking Mormons come round the door, I'm not saying BE A SAINT, I'm just saying clear up the fucking Chinese takeaway. I'm not even saying clear up the last Chinese takeaway, I'm saying clear up the last Chinese takeaway but three. Or four would do.

ALICE suddenly sits bolt upright. Her hair is unkempt. She is sleeping in a grey-white singlet. There are dark rings around her eyes. She is staring with her mouth open. SANDY stares back at her. A silence. Then she collapses back without a sound and turns over.

I mean even my mum clears up a bit! Nothing extreme, washing windows and that, nothing WILD, ironing underpants and that, but not even my mum, fucking slag she is and all, not even my mum lets something what's dripped go mouldy on the fucking TV screen . . . there is something what's dripped and gone mouldy on the fucking TV screen, I mean what are you trying to do, make A POINT? I mean, you watch the TV news, all the fucking time, all channels, channel hopping, same news over and over, I mean what is it with you, do you like to see what's going on in the fucking world through a smear of stuck-on sweet 'n' sour pork? I mean you are driving me mad, do you know that? Right I've decided, say nothing, I'll clear up the fucking TV screen myself, right? (*He is lost at how to do so. He returns to the attack.*) And where WAS you last night anyway? Me stuck here, waiting . . . I even watched the FUCKING NEWS for you . . . some fucking super gun . . . going in and out of some fucking country or other, Greece, Israel, Iran . . . I tried to remember, but I don't know foreign places, they just don't stick, I just don't know 'em, in't nowhere on the map 'cept ENGLAND far as I'm concerned . . . And anyway fell asleep, didn't I . . . right . . . clear up the . . . Right how do I do that? (*He pauses.*) Need a little aerosol can of something to clean something, don't you, yeah, a can. (*He kicks at the mess. He stumbles. He picks up some newspaper. He tears it, making a wad. He looks around again and picks up an open lager can. It is empty. Then he finds a can with beer still in it. He wets the wad of newspaper with the beer. He goes to wipe the television screen. But he notices the wires leading to the television and video machine. They are botched together with insulating tape. The tape hangs ragged at a join. He touches the join. He receives an electric shock. The wire sticks to his fingers for a second.*) Aaaaaaaargh! (*He crouches. He is shivering. He retches and –*)

Aside No. 1. 'Little Chinese Box'

(*NB: in these asides to the audience the stage is transformed. Sharp lighting with strong shadows.*)

SANDY.

Hits you
    desire
        not
For sex
    that's there
        rain or shine
no – desire

      for THINGS, it
            hits you –
MINE MINE
      you kind
            of scream inside
Make that MINE –

Saw this ad
      Sunday Express
            magazine
Special offer
      limited
            edition
Ninety quid
      for this
            little Chinese
Box, a dragon
      on the lid
            glittering
Gold and green
      trick locks
            As made
for Chinese
      Emperors
            THOUSANDS of years
Ago
      a beautiful
            tiny, shiny
Box, marquetry
      all intricate
            all inlaid
tears ran down my face
      I was burning up I wanted
            it, very very HARD

BUT got
      no credit
            card
Have I! And
      it's 'send
            no cash'
Got no Visa
      No American Express
            to flash
Got no poncy access

To the high life
           have I

All the special offers
           bone china
                statuettes
Specially minted coins
           in commemorated sets
                are not for me

Look! no bank
           account, no
                cheque book
Got
           no
                right
HOW DO THEY THINK
           I LIVE, BY A TRICK
                OF THE LIGHT?

   A pause.

Little Chinese box
           secret locks
                tiny in my hand
I'd wrap you up
           in a clean cloth
                a thing from a magic land.

   Change: the scene is restored and continues.

SANDY (*saliva drips from his mouth. The shivering is worse. He hugs himself. He controls the shivering. He floods with fury*). Right! Right! Want the fucking news do you, all channels, here's the fucking news. (*He picks the television up and smashes it to the ground. There is a muffled bang as the tube implodes. There is a little smoke. It is dust. The sleepers do not stir. He is near tears.*) I mean I love you, you fucking stupid cow, you're going to kill yourself, you know that, I mean no one'll care, no one'll know, and one of these crazy nights you're going to take something down you and NOT HANDLE IT, you'll end up with your tongue back of your throat, yeah, one of these crazy nights of yours . . . (*He pauses.*) Yeah one of these nights some face'll do you over . . . and there you'll be, in the street, choked on your own sick or something. And they'll scrape you up, they'll slam you in King's College mortuary and not even know your name, it'll be 'Jane Smith'

then three days later WHAM, up to West Norwood
crematorium and 'PUFF', smoke, thank you very much, fucking
cremated . . . I know! It happened to a black geezer I knew,
unknown corpse, WHAM PUFF thank-you-very-much
cremated, 'fore anyone got to know he'd even died, not even a
fucking rose bush at West Norwood fucking crematorium to
prove he'd ever existed on the fucking planet . . . (*He is in tears.*)
A very South London kind of death, and coming your way, my
love, you stupid slag cunt, I can't take it no more, I'm going
back and see if my mum's there . . . (*He is holding his stomach. He
looks at her. He pauses. He grabs a hold-all. He looks in it. He looks
about for his possessions. He kicks at the mess. He gives up and goes to
the door. He exits, slamming the door behind him.*)

*The window shakes. Nothing happens. A grinding sound. The top
segment of the window slips down with a crash. The sleepers do not stir.
Nothing happens. Then SANDY appears in the gap of the broken
window.*

You're doing this deliberately, in't you! You want me to feel
fucking helpless, don't you! It is fucking unfair, did I or did I
not say get the fucking Town Hall on this? I said, ring the
fucking wank pit at the Housing Department, did I or did I
not? (*A pause.*) Alice, WAKE UP. (*A pause.*) Right! I've decided,
say nothing, I'll fix the fucking window myself, right? (*He is
lost.*) Right how do I do that? (*He pauses.*) Need a bit of glass,
measured up, and a dollop of putty, yeah . . . I'll see if I can
get a bit of board. Yeah, nails and that.

He exits.

2.

ALICE *sits bolt upright. She pulls a blanket around her. She closes her
eyes.* JOANNE *sits bolt upright. Her hair is dyed jet black in the manner
of a Goth. When she comes to dress, her clothes are Gothette.*

   ALICE *stares at her.*

ALICE (*click into the story that runs in her head and which she sees very
   strongly*). What do the lovers have for breakfast? On the 'plane?
   In the morning, first class, Cathay Pacific? Looking down, at
   the sea, six miles below? (*Click out of it.*)

JOANNE. 'Scuse us . . .

   But ALICE *stands and returns to stare at the television set.*

ALICE. The television has had an accident.

JOANNE. 'Scuse us . . .

ALICE. Where's the radio? (*To* JOANNE.) Or was the radio
nicked? (*A pause, staring at* JOANNE.) Why do I think you
nicked the radio?

> JOANNE *is lost.* ALICE *stares at her.* JOANNE *looks at the
> television.*

Did YOU nick the radio?

JOANNE. I don't know.

ALICE. You don't know. (*She shrugs. She mutters, sing-song.*) What
do you know, what do I know, no, most of us . . . (*Cod South
London.*) 'dunno nuphink'. (*Click.*) Why, they have orange juice
and croissant and black coff-coff-coffee, and a little plastic pot
of marmalade and a mop, roll-mop stuck with a little cocktail
stick. (*Click. To* JOANNE.) Don't they, on the 'plane? She and
Sylvester? (*Realises she's said that.*) Oh.

JOANNE. I . . . (*Then doggedly.*) Round the back of Waterloo
Station, wan't I.

ALICE (*she stares at* JOANNE *again*). You flogged my Hitachi,
round the back of Waterloo Station?

JOANNE. Maybe.

ALICE. 'Maybe' you stole my radio and flogged it round the back
of Waterloo Station?

JOANNE. I'm only trying to help.

ALICE (*stares at the floor. She is still for a moment, then moves*). TV
AM will be over now, AND BBC Breakfast Time . . . but
maybe BBC Two will have a newsflash. If they know more
about the super gun. (*She stares down at the smashed television set. It
is as if she has not seen it a moment ago. She realises she has. She
scrabbles about in the mess and finds a can of lager. She opens it and
drinks.*)

> *Meanwhile* JOANNE *has picked up a framed photograph from the
> debris and is staring at it.*

I'm the toddler. Four, I was four, right?

JOANNE *persists in staring at the photograph.*

(*She is irritated.*) The older girl is my sister Rosa. The shrub in a pot is a shrub in a pot. The creosote fence is a creosote fence. And the strong little woman with the tied-back hair is our mother, right?

JOANNE *is inert.* ALICE *snatches the photograph and tosses it into the debris.* ALICE *stares at the wall. She is still for a moment. Then she moves. She catches* JOANNE *looking at her.*

I'm not flashing. I'm not. Look, do you mind me bringing this up? Who are you?

Nothing from JOANNE.

Do I know you? Or, do you know me?

JOANNE. My name's Joanne. Your name's Alice Brine.

ALICE. How do you know that?

JOANNE. You told me last night.

ALICE. Ridiculous. *(Glares at her.)* Did you flog the kettle too?

JOANNE. Only been here once, han't I.

ALICE. When?

JOANNE. Now.

ALICE. Oh?

JOANNE. You asked me back.

ALICE. Never!

JOANNE. Last night.

ALICE *(pauses)*. Did I?

JOANNE. That's the trouble, doing dust.

ALICE. What?

JOANNE. You get flashes.

ALICE *(with a natural laugh)*. Yes.

JOANNE. Turn a strange corner.

ALICE. What?

JOANNE. That's what my mum says. 'Don't you turn a strange corner.' Though she don't mean drugs. She means, you know, life.

ALICE *stares at* JOANNE *then she goes on to all fours. She rummages in the debris.* JOANNE *attempts to ask a question.*

Wh . . . Wh . . . No.

ALICE *(pulling an electric flex out of the debris).* Kettle! *(The flex is long. There are two extensions. It ends with exposed wires.)* No kettle.

JOANNE. It was you. You was round the back of Waterloo.

ALICE *stares at her.*

(She finds it difficult to speak.) You had a radio and a kettle.

ALICE. Was it electric?

JOANNE. Yeah.

ALICE. Oh then it must have been me.

JOANNE *(she is puzzled. She tries again).* It was a barter.

ALICE. What?

JOANNE. Barter. Off this face.

ALICE. You're being ridiculous.

JOANNE. You wanted a barter, off this face. You had a radio and a kettle, in a bag.

ALICE. There was no bag! Because I was not! Round the back of Waterloo!

They both look at a dirty but brightly coloured shopping bag lying in the debris. A pause.

JOANNE. He wan't having none. He wanted a fuck.

ALICE. Who wanted a fuck?

JOANNE. This face. You wanted a barter, the radio and the kettle for dust, but he wan't having none. He wanted a fuck.

ALICE. A fuck AND the radio and the electric kettle?

JOANNE. He must've thought you was clean, what with you being middle class.

ALICE. Thanks very much. *(She pauses.)* Did we hit him? *(She remembers.)* I hit him. Oh Gawd. In his eye. *(She flicks her hand.)* His eye! On my finger! And the way he just . . . curled up at our feet.

JOANNE. Don't worry. He was a scumbag.

ALICE *(bright)*. Oh good, that's alright then. *(Then unsteady, the memory of the night catching up with her.)* I don't go down to Waterloo to do that, you know, I mean not a lot. I was just desperate, you know. *(A forced giggle, it fades. She lights a cigarette and sucks it, her hand shaky. She uses the lager can as an ashtray.)* Still! 'Be streetwise' in your city. Know every mark on your own bit of piss-soaked wall. Go armed in your mind, ready to mutilate. *(This has no effect on JOANNE. ALICE eyes her.)* You from round here?

JOANNE *(cautiously)*. Croydon.

ALICE. Oh Croydon! More distant than the Moon. We inner city dwellers have to wear a space suit to go to Croydon, the air is so thin.

JOANNE *(jammed)*. W . . . W . . . W . . .

ALICE *(dressing)*. I've got to get the papers. The news, it's a need. *(And a false brightness.)* So! You're a runaway? Was your dad getting in your knickers?

JOANNE *stares at her.*

Or just knocking you about?

JOANNE. No!

For a few moments ALICE argues with herself. Then she returns to the questions.

ALICE. Your mum was on the game then?

JOANNE. No . . . *(Shocked.)* No!

ALICE. Boyfriend, is it? What's wrong with him? Drugs? Violence? Gay?

JOANNE *(she pauses. She becomes distressed. She mumbles)*. It's nothing, it's me.

ALICE. What?

JOANNE *(she shouts)*. It's nothing, it's me! *(Then quietly.)* I got this weepiness.

ALICE. Weepiness.

JOANNE. Yeah.

ALICE *(a moment, then ALICE realises)*. A vaginal discharge?

JOANNE. From inside. It's horrible.

ALICE. Yes?

JOANNE. And I couldn't tell him.

ALICE. Your boyfriend . . .

JOANNE. I couldn't tell him.

ALICE. Why not, for gawdsake?

JOANNE. He'd be upset.

ALICE. What do you mean HE'd be upset?

JOANNE. It would break him up.

ALICE *stares at her.*

He'd just go to pieces. No way could I tell him.

ALICE. For crying out loud . . . all that we've said the past twenty, twenty-five years . . . Joanne, screw HIS feelings, what about YOU, what about YOUR body, YOUR place in the world, what YOU want . . . *(To herself.)* Has everything got to be said over and over again, from scratch, every generation of every kid getting VD from some bloke? Oh what the hell, what what what . . . it's all gone to pieces . . . now it's all scribbling on a wall, no one notices, they just walk on by . . . *(To* JOANNE.) What about your mum? Did you tell her?

JOANNE. Nah. My mum's a cleaner.

ALICE. What, you mean she's just not there? Office cleaning, all night, early morning . . .

JOANNE *(hating having to explain)*. Nah! She cleans. The house. All the time. She goes mad for it. She's got the pages of the Daily Express on the chairs and that. She irons it.

ALICE. Irons?

JOANNE. The Daily Express. So it's clean when she puts it on the chairs. Dirt in the house'd kill my mum.

ALICE. Dirt like you? That what you mean? You ran away, so you'd not muck up your mother's Daily Express with a dose of the clap?

JOANNE *stares at her, then begins to dress.*

Have you been to a doctor? To a clinic?

JOANNE *squirms away, pulling at her clothes.*

No don't GO. That would be DUMB, to go back under the Bridge when you're sick.

JOANNE. I got somewhere to go!

ALICE. Fine! Where?

JOANNE *(looks at the floor. She is tight-lipped)*. South. *(And continues to dress.)*

ALICE. South.

JOANNE. I said, South.

ALICE. What, Brighton?

JOANNE. Just South.

ALICE. Don't get into the Brighton scene. Brighton's hit rock bottom for runaways. It's used needles floating on the little waves, lapping the pebbles.

JOANNE. Not Brighton, South!

ALICE. Why isn't there an original way of going to pieces, a unique path of degeneration? Must it always be drugs, booze, STDs and bad men?

JOANNE *takes a step back.*

Alright! Tell me . . . no I'll tell you. You're sleeping rough, having run away from your mum, dad, boyfriend and now you're waiting the while for this new guy you've met, what, in a park in a club, and, what, you and he are going SOUTH? And he's gone off somewhere, what, NORTH? For a couple of days, gone NORTH to fix some dosh, some vast amount of money that he's owed by SOME FACE in, where, Salford? And then, what, he'll be back for you and you'll be off, to the great land that lies to the South of the known world.

JOANNE. Avignon, actually.

ALICE. Avignon.

JOANNE. It's a town in France.

ALICE. No it's not.

JOANNE *(a slight hesitation)*. It's in the South of France . . .

ALICE. It's a town in your head. With . . . glass walls, palace gardens, fountains, only in your head. It's looking into the Christmas tree when you're a kid, and seeing a fairy land, dark green and glitter. It's in your head! *(To herself.)* Avignon, in our heads. *(To* JOANNE.) Is he foreign?

JOANNE *stares.*

The guy you're going to Avignon with.

JOANNE. He's Dutch.

ALICE. Of course he is! VERY, VERY Dutch. Six foot six, hair in a pony tail, deep voice . . . good English, suntan and oh, very very clear eyes despite all the drugs he does. Is he strong-legged? Strange how continental young men have over-developed legs. Like pectorals on their inner thighs. Urrgh . . .

JOANNE. Don't know about that. His name's John.

ALICE. He's a pimp.

JOANNE. He's not!

ALICE. The Danish John, the Dutch John, always he is a pimp.

JOANNE. He's not! *(She hesitates.)* He's a Buddhist.

ALICE. Oh gawd.

JOANNE. He's a mime artist. We're going to do mime.

ALICE. Mime.

JOANNE. There's a whole circuit. We do Amsterdam, outside Central Station. Then Brussels. Paris, the Beaubourg Square. Germany, outside Cologne Cathedral. Then France to Avignon. For a Festival. There'll be hundreds of us, John's told me, people like him and me meeting down there, from all over . . . *(She dries up.)*

ALICE. And are you a good mime 'artiste'?

JOANNE. You just do what you feel.

ALICE. What a disgusting habit.

ALICE *smirks.* JOANNE *suppresses a laugh. A sudden relaxation between them.*

JOANNE. I'm good at it. I mean I could be good at it.

ALICE. Why not be good at it?

JOANNE. Yeah! Course I'll just collect the money off the crowd, at first, while I learn.

ALICE. And what is the mime about?

JOANNE. It's about the nuclear holocaust.

ALICE. Original. Originality is meant to be all in art. Unlike in life.

JOANNE. It happens after it.

ALICE. After the nuclear . . .

JOANNE. It's symbolic.

ALICE. I'll miss The Bomb, now the Russians have given up. Having Armageddon just a second away, for all those years . . . it concentrated the mind. What have we got to replace it? AIDS doesn't really do the job, does it, as an inspiring apocalypse. Have you told Dutch John you've got an infection?

JOANNE *shakes her head. She cannot speak.*

ALICE *(to herself).* Oh gawd look at you, another little mousey innocent, getting sick in the walls. *(To* JOANNE.) How many mice do you think there are in London? How many die, every day? *(Suddenly angry.)* How many, tucked away in corners of the city, tiny skeletons turning into dust? Who's counting?

JOANNE *shrugs.*

YOU. Who's counting YOU?

JOANNE *(off* ALICE's *anger, pulling at her clothes).* Don't know!

ALICE. No one's counting you, you little slag.

JOANNE. Right!

ALICE. No one!

JOANNE. Right I got it! *(She is dressed.)*

ALICE *(click).* She picks up the little Cathay Pacific bag, she leads him to the toilet at the back, the stewardess is off down the aisle . . . and in they slip, lock the door, and she wiggles her panties down, perches her bum up on the little aluminium sink, her bum's like mine, 'we going to do this?' says he, all shy, but GET OUT OF THIS ALICE, AM I GOING THROUGH WITH THIS . . .

JOANNE *(taking a step back).* I . . .

ALICE. . . . Sylvester and me, I me, I, high above the Pacific Ocean . . .

She is getting frightened. She clutches JOANNE.

But the little Cathay Pacific bag ... NO ... bulges ... No ...
Cries, little baby baby fingers at the zip ALICE NO ... I hit
the man in the face he hits me, my face, all squashy on the
little loo mirror ... Flush it away, pummel it, squash down the
aluminium loo, fall down baby into the sea, OH SHIT, no
flight only fall, oh, oh, oh, oh, oh, oh, oh. *(Click. She stares at*
JOANNE.)

JOANNE *forces* ALICE *away with considerable strength.*

JOANNE. If you do mime, you're strong. Strength's the secret. So
don't you. Don't you do nothing.

ALICE. No. I mean ... *(She pauses. She is worn out.)* Just hang
around for a couple of days. After Easter, go down to King's
College Hospital. There's a women's clinic ...

JOANNE *(recoiling)*. No way ...

ALICE. It's no hassle, all women, the clinic's a very female world.

JOANNE. No way ...

ALICE. It won't be the plague, promise. It'll be something
simple, something they can still handle ...

JOANNE *shakes her head.*

(She shakes her head and wipes her eyes.) But you've got to tell
Dutch John.

JOANNE. I don't need this shit.

ALICE *(to herself, angrily)*. I'm doing good. I am. Oh shit! *(To*
JOANNE.) It's a PAIN IN THE BUM, but with diseases it's
always down to the woman to tell the man. What about
another little Joanne, the Dutchman's miming with, right now
in Salford?

JOANNE. Don't know why you go on about Salford. He's not in
Salford. *(She hesitates.)* He's in Liverpool.

ALICE. Gawd, when he gets back hose him down with Dettol.
Oh Sod it! *(She rushes at the pile of screwed-up papers. She goes on all
fours. She flings the mess around. Then she finds a bulging and battered
paper file. She opens it. She throws papers out of the file in a fury. She
finds a card.)* The King's clinic number.

She flicks the card at JOANNE. JOANNE *makes no move to pick it up.* ALICE *stands and picks the card up. The following action flares suddenly.* ALICE *grabs* JOANNE. JOANNE *struggles. With a crazy impulse* ALICE *attempts to put the card in* JOANNE's *mouth.* JOANNE *pummels her.* ALICE *succeeds in putting the card down* JOANNE's *T shirt. They back away from each other. A pause.*

I'm going to get the papers. Be here or not, it's up to you. *(A pause.)* If you want to make some instant, put a saucepan on the electric. If there is some instant.

She opens her bag. She is suddenly very nervous. She drops the bag. She picks it up. She takes out a purse. She checks there is some money. They look at each other. ALICE *goes off quickly.*

3.

Joanne's Mime.

She is thrown to the floor.
She springs to all fours looking about her.
She goes around the four walls of a cell.
She feels the bars.
She beats the bars in a rage.
She collapses within herself.

She pauses.

She sits on a stool and is still.
She looks up at the ceiling.
She sees a hook which she describes with her hand.
She stands and tries to reach it.
She moves the stool and stands on it beneath the hook.
She removes a belt.
She tries to prevent her trousers falling.
She gives up trying to prevent her trousers falling.
She ties a loop in the end of the belt.
She slings the loop at the hook.
She fails on the first attempt, she succeeds on the second.
She pulls the belt to check that it is secure.
She tightens the belt about her neck.

She pauses.

She kicks the stool away and dangles as her body turns with her face away from us.
She leans her head to one side in the study of a hanged body.
She spins and comes to rest with her face towards us.

She flits her eyes from side to side.

JOANNF. Think 'sod this for a load of bananas'.

> *She grasps the belt above her head.*
> *She pulls her body up with a great effort.*
> *She portrays terrible strain.*
> *She floods her face with a ghastly grimace of triumph.*
> *Then she speaks without any strain at all.*

If you're going to make this work, the trick's to be free inside. Inside what you do. Then you'll kid everyone you're nearly dead.

4.

'BERTIE' pushes the door open and comes on. He is dressed conservatively in a good quality businessman's suit and coat. He carries a black chunky briefcase. He holds his hands politely before him. He stands still.
JOANNE spins slowly in her mime and sees him. 'BERTIE''s English is excellent. His German accent gives his speech an even formality.

'BERTIE'. Rappacini, is it not? *(A pause.)* Giuseppe Rappacini, the father of the mime of the hanged man.

Nothing from JOANNE. She holds her position in her mime.

Are you familiar with his Eternal Mountaineer? The mime ascends the mountainside by a rope, pulling forward, then slipping back, forever. So simple, so banal. Yet Rappacini's spectators would laugh until they wept, and weep until they laughed again, no? Italian histrionics, a circus culture, all fire and sentimentality. Miss Alice Brine? *(A pause.)* I am a friend of your sister. From Berlin. Rosa gave me your address.

JOANNE, still holding herself in the mime. She stares at him. A flicker of fatigue from 'BERTIE'.

You are not Alice. You are too young. But I am at the right apartment? *(His eye darts over the mess in the room.)* Are these conditions representative of British working-class housing?

SANDY enters, barging the door open. He struggles to carry a large piece of plywood. It is covered by aerosoled graffiti.

SANDY. Right I am fucking doing this, this one is down to me, I am sorting this one. I am doing this one temporarily, fucking once and for all. *(He looks from JOANNE to 'BERTIE'.)* What are you?

'BERTIE'. I am a friend of Miss Brine's sister . . .

SANDY. Yeah? Cat bring you in, or what?

'BERTIE' *tenses, then smiles at the idiom.*

'BERTIE'. Ah! The cat's dinner, an animal from the field, blood and fur on the hausfrau's clean kitchen floor . . . *(Looking about the room.)* Yes.

SANDY *(to* JOANNE). What about you? You what, came back with Alice last night? Thought there was something, dragged along.

'BERTIE'. I have just arrived in London. I am from Berlin.

SANDY *(ignoring* 'BERTIE' *and having difficulty with the piece of board).* Typical bloody Alice, back with something tied to her, dragged along, nothing personal darling, I get fucking sick of it. Still, got an hammer and some nails from my mum's, my old dad's, not that HE ever banged a fucking nail while HE was around. *(To* 'BERTIE'. 'Scuse me friend. *(He loses control. He bangs the piece of wood down against the wall. He slips and bangs his head. He turns over sitting with his legs splayed out. He rubs his head.)*

Why is getting ANYTHING FUCKING DONE AT ALL so fucking hard, fucking glass, fucking tellies blowing out and fucking wood, nails, hammer . . . I mean windows falling out, walls coming down, damp coming up, damp's coming up at my mum's and all, I mean it's all fucking running to fucking stand still.

'BERTIE'. Goethe said 'Genius is ninety-nine percent perspiration, one percent inspiration.'

SANDY *stares at him.*

That can apply to the simplest task of daily life.

SANDY *stares.*

I once built a house, of wood. A whole house! In the countryside, in the forest.

SANDY. ?

'BERTIE'. For the summers. It was not large, but there was a verandah, to sit out on fine evenings. I was proud of that verandah, stupidly so. *(Suddenly hard. A fist rather than a finger pointed at* SANDY.) Alice's sister will be in London. She will very very much want see me. Tell Alice this, please. I will call again. You are clear?

SANDY, *his mouth slightly open.*

(He turns to JOANNE.) Does your clown end hanged?

JOANNE *completes her mime. She raises one foot. She sinks slowly down onto her behind. She raises both feet and grips the belt with her ankles and feet. Her hands are now free. She frees her neck from the belt. She goes into a handstand. She does a back flip and is standing.* 'BERTIE' *smiles.*

A pretty escape.

JOANNE. What . . . *(Struggles.)* What . . . *(Gives up.)* I don't know your name.

'BERTIE' *pauses for a moment. Then with an ironic little Prussian bow and clip of the heels.*

'BERTIE'. 'Bertolt Brecht'. *(He turns. To* SANDY.) Put this on with brass screws, not nails. For the weather. *(Low.)* 'For fucksake', 'friend'.

He exits. A pause. JOANNE *pays no attention to him as he speaks.*

SANDY. What was he pushing, then? Hunh! *(A scoff. A pause.)* People coming right up to you, from all ways, pushing something, after something, AT you, push sell, push sell . . . Street, pub, bus stop, top of the bus, then IN through your fucking front door . . . THEY COME RIGHT UP TO YOU, push sell, push sell . . .

He pauses. His anger has made him breathless. JOANNE *stands with her hand to her mouth lost in her thoughts. And* SANDY *is off again.*

I mean, these days, no one does nothing for fucking LOVE, no one does nothing for the fucking HELL OF IT . . . and when you do . . . turns out you can't do it without FUCKING BRASS SCREWS.

JOANNE *practises a moment from the mime. She is self-absorbed.* SANDY *watches her with his mouth open.* JOANNE *stands still.* SANDY *stands with a grunt. With further grunts he attempts to measure the width of the window and the width of the piece of the wood with his arms held out. The wood is too wide. He kicks it. Then he draws a line with his fingers trying to judge where a cut should be. He stands back looking at the wood.* JOANNE *makes a mime movement hesitantly but stops. She shakes her head.*

ALICE *enters quickly. She carries a wodge of the tabloid daily papers beneath her arm. She throws them down. She kneels. She grabs the 'Daily Express'.*

ALICE. 'DOOMSDAY GUN: HOW IRAQ DUPED BRITAIN . . .' *(She rips through the pages. She throws the paper away. She grabs 'The Sun'.)* 'BLOODY FRENCH SINK OUR HOLS. Bloody-minded French air traffic men will start today to wreck thousands of Britons' Easter holidays.' *(She rips through the pages then throws the paper away. She grabs 'The Sport'. She rips through the pages.)* 'EASTER BUNNIES. It's the time when we all go bonkers'. *(She rips through the pages.)* 'SEX ORGY PERIL OF BONKERS ELBOW'. *(She throws the paper away. SANDY reaches for it.)*

SANDY. That the Sport?

She slaps his hand hard. He recoils.

ALICE *(she grabs the 'Daily Mirror').* 'The riddle of the "giant nuclear gun" exploded into a war of words last night.' *(She looks down the page.)* TOPLESS DEBBIE'S SKYLARK'. *(She rips through the pages then throws the paper away. She is breathless.)*

SANDY *(to* JOANNE*)*. She thinks she's going to be in there.

ALICE *(to* JOANNE*)*. Did that LUMP say something?

JOANNE, *lost. She shrugs.*

SANDY *(to* JOANNE*)*. In the news. She thinks she's going to be an horror story in there.

ALICE *(to* JOANNE*)*. Shall I speak to it? It is very much in its own ENVELOPE of understanding, a plastic shopping bag is drawn TIGHT about its TIGHT little brain. Shall I try, nevertheless?

JOANNE *shrugs.*

(To SANDY*.)* Sandy? What . . . is . . . that . . . wood?

SANDY *(to* JOANNE*)*. She han't got no reason to think she's going to be. An horror story.

ALICE *(to* JOANNE*)*. Still, he has a tight little bum.

SANDY *(to* JOANNE*)*. She thinks the pigs are onto her, fucking reporters. But it's all madness.

ALICE *(to* JOANNE*)*. Don't you think he has a tight little bum?

It compensates for the TIGHT LITTLE BRAIN.

SANDY *(to* JOANNE). Fucking MADNESS she's got . . .

ALICE *(to* JOANNE). But the lump loves me. He doth. He's love sick. The 'Sauph Lundun' swain doth lie, swooning in his pool of lager. For me! Me!

SANDY *(to* JOANNE). WHY? WHY do people go to pieces? Fucking happening all over. Tearing 'emselves to bits, I mean why do they BOTHER? She's got a great job and all. Social worker . . .

JOANNE *starts.*

ALICE. I said, what is that filthy stupid wood?

JOANNE *(to* ALICE, *angrily).* You didn't say you was the scum.

SANDY. It's not wood it's a bit of board!

ALICE. Oh BOARD, BOARD . . .

JOANNE. You didn't say you was the fucking social scum.

SANDY. Oh board, fucking hardboard.

ALICE. 'Course a lump of manly man knows what's WOOD and what's BOARD . . .

JOANNE. Slagging round Waterloo. Crawling all over us, spying on us . . .

ALICE *(to* JOANNE). Don't you worry your pretty little head, I am conducting a kind of EXPERIMENT IN LIVING, OK?

SANDY. I'll sort of re-do the graffiti . . . What do you think?

ALICE *(to* JOANNE). Oh, it's taking up art!

SANDY. Should the fucker go inside or outside?

ALICE *(to* JOANNE). The witless LUMP, is going to be an ARTIST, and attempt to disrupt the contemporary world.

JOANNE *(to* ALICE). Joanne's not my name. Don't think I went and gived you my name. You don't know nothing about me.

SANDY. What are you doing, what do you want, grief out o' every little fucking thing?

ALICE *(to herself).* Every little thing, every little grain . . .

JOANNE. You say this is some kind of experiment. I don't want to be no experiment.

ALICE *is startled. She looks at* JOANNE.

Social scum experiment. You lot is always down under the
Bridge, experimenting on us. Doing questions, questionnaires.
And TV cameras. There's always TV cameras down under the
Bridge, doing programmes. They always interview this girl
called Sandra, 'cos she looks really great, really fucking
homeless. Cold sores on her mouth and like she's twelve years
old. Though really she's eighteen. And she tarts up the cold
sores with make-up. And charges the TV fifty quid an
interview. She's not even dossing at all. She lives with a face at
the Oval called Jimmy.

ALICE *and* SANDY *stare at her.*

And I'm not homeless and all, don't you call me that. You got
no right, to slag me off and call me that. I got a home. Here.
(She hits her chest.) Me. This is where I live. In here.

ALICE. Bully for you. When I said experiment I . . . Look, I'm a
bother junky, right? I am trying very hard not TO CARE.

SANDY. I fucking HATE it when you talk like this.

ALICE *(ignoring him).* I try NOT TO CARE one day at a time. I
am trying to give up other people's . . . poisoned lives, running
through my veins.

JOANNE. You oughtn't a live like this, that's all.

ALICE. WHAT?

JOANNE. Not if you work for the scum. You oughtn't a live in
this shit.

And ALICE *and* JOANNE, *screaming at each other.*

ALICE. I want to live in this shit!

JOANNE. It in't right!

SANDY. Look I broke the window . . .

They do not hear him.

ALICE. Oh I see! We must be goody-goody two-shoes in white
coats and live in white rooms, with white walls, and above all
PROFESSIONAL, always there! For when you get splattered
on the walls, when you get homeless, get diseased, get drugged
up, fucked up, splattered on the walls . . . we have to BE

THERE to scrape up what's left of you . . . 'cos we are the Social Services!

JOANNE. It just in't right!

SANDY *(pulling the wood toward the door)*. I'll do it with nails . . .

ALICE. You think people like me will always be there, don't you, as this country slides into THE TOILET . . .

SANDY *(desperate now, for* ALICE *to stop her riff)*. Yeah, with nails, you got to fucking make do, let live and let live, fucking brass screws or not.

ALICE. Well little Jo-Jo,, this is not a stable world . . . the goody-goodies are coming down to join you . . . YUP! This is the revolt of 'the goody-goodies', 'cos we are GIVING UP!

SANDY. I could bop someone when you talk like this, really fucking BOP SOMEONE . . . There's got to be someone to bop, just point me in the right fucking direction . . . *(Repeatedly.)* BOP! BOP! BOP!

SANDY *slews the board into the mess of the room. He kicks it. He pulls the ironing board over.* ALICE *grabs him round the waist. They struggle with* SANDY *continuing his 'BOP BOP BOP' wrecking spree and* ALICE *trying to restrain him.* JOANNE *attempts to pull the two apart. The three of them fall into the debris. They are still.* SANDY, *running down.*

BOP! Bop . . . bop.

They are breathless. A pause.

ALICE *(to* JOANNE). Did you find the instant coffee?

JOANNE. Not really.

SANDY. Watch yourself! There's a live wire.

JOANNE *moves.*

Watch yourself!

They are stuck. The three of them look about cautiously. The door is pushed open. Enter ROSA. *She wears a dark coat over a conservative two-piece suit. Her clothes are dowdy but well cleaned. She carries a large and battered suitcase. She has a shoulder bag.* ROSA *looks at the scene before her, fixated and appalled. A silence. Then* ALICE, SANDY *and* JOANNE *break into giggles.*

ALICE. Folks, this is my sister Rosa. From Berlin.

ALICE *corpses.* ROSA *is dead still.* ALICE, SANDY *and* JOANNE *rein their giggling in. Then* ROSA *swings her shoulder bag round. She takes out a lump of concrete. There are coloured aerosol marks on it.*

ROSA. I brought you a present.

ROSA leans over them and offers the concrete to ALICE. ALICE *will not take it. A puzzled* SANDY *does.*

It's a bit of the wall.

SANDY. What wall?

Suddenly ALICE *stands and rushes past* ROSA *to the door. A blackout.*

ACT TWO

Saturday, April 14th, 1990.

The flat is radically cleared up. The old newspapers are straightened out and in neat piles. ROSA's suitcase is opened in a corner. Its contents are neat. The smashed television and video are stacked to one side. There is a neat pile of all the breakages. There is a rolled-up carpet. There is a mop and a bucket with a packet of cleaning powder and two bottles of Dettol disinfectant. There is a box-shaped packet of concentrated New Ariel.

1.

ROSA *and* SANDY *are busy working on the room. Together they are putting up improvised curtains. A corner of the room is still uncleared.* ROSA *still wears her suit but with the top removed and a tea towel tucked into her waist.* SANDY *is wearing a pinafore. It has German writing on it. There is a broom and a mop.* ROSA *picks up the broom and sweeps.* SANDY *steps back and admires the curtains.*

SANDY. Rosa, is these fucking curtains rubbish? I can't tell the fuck whether they are or not.

    ROSA *closes her eyes blanching at his swearing.* SANDY, *contemplating the curtains.*

    I mean, should be sort of ... BUNCHY, didn't they ... sort of SEWN UP down the fucking bottom ... Be great to have a little string and all, to pull 'em fucking shut and that.

ROSA. It's the best we can do.

SANDY. Nah ... this is all fucking ace of you, Rosa. Here ... let's put the carpet down ...

ROSA. Later. *(She stops sweeping. She puts her finger on a point on the wall.)* Put a nail in the wall, here.

SANDY. Oh, right. *(He retrieves his hammer and nails enthusiastically. He bangs a nail into the wall as he talks.)* Got a picture have you? All the way from ...

ROSA. East Berlin.

SANDY. Berlin, yeah fucking brighten it up in here, give you something to look at, little country scene . . . or yachts or something. *(Banging in a nail clumsily.)* Yeah, fucking ace, Rosa . . . getting out shopping first thing, getting stuck in, giving the place a going over . . . *(He bends the nail.)* Oh fuck!

He pulls the nail out with the claw of the hammer. He begins again. ROSA, *waiting patiently.*

I mean it's what I been wanting to do round here for yonks, but it's not down to the bloke is it.

ROSA. No?

SANDY. It's the woman's touch, in't it. You can't move without that.

ROSA. No?

SANDY. Was it alright, staying the night at my mum's?

ROSA. Fine.

SANDY. Looked after you did she? Fucking talk a lot?

ROSA *(it was clearly an awful night)*. She was very kind.

SANDY. Fucking yackitty-yacked you to death.

ROSA. No no.

SANDY *(eyeing her. He's worried)*. So it was alright, in my mum's other room?

ROSA. Yes.

SANDY. Couldn't have you staying the night in the fucking shit here, could we.

ROSA. Alice didn't come back here last night?

SANDY *(a brief pause. Then angrily)*. Slag me off rotten, did she, my fucking old mum?

ROSA *(irritated)*. I'm sure your mother loves you very much. She said you were a very . . . very WILLING son.

SANDY. You what?

ROSA *(indicating the wall)*. Shall we . . .

SANDY. Yeah. *(He lines the nail up. Then looks at her.)* You married then?

ROSA *(she gives him a hard look)*. Guess.

SANDY. You're married.

ROSA. And WHY do you think I'm married?

SANDY. The way you clear things up.

ROSA *(low)*. My God.

SANDY *(hits his thumb with the hammer)*. Fucking cunt hammer! *(He shakes his hand continuing to speak.)* No, Alice will be over the moon when she gets back, and all.

ROSA. She wasn't here at all last night, was she?

SANDY. Don't worry, she'll be back any time now. *(Steps back from the wall.)* One nail.

ROSA *goes to her suitcase. She takes out a crucifix. She hangs it on the nail.* SANDY *is nonplussed.*

Very nice.

ROSA *(turns away. She starts to sort out the mess in the corner of the room)*. We should air those mattresses.

SANDY. What?

ROSA. Put them outside. In the air.

SANDY. You can't put nothing outside round here. Get fucking nicked in one second flat. *(His face shines.)* I know what we want here! One of them squirters, them clear the air aerosols . . . you know, smells of fucking pine trees. Yeah, we could spray the mattresses with that, give the fuckers a good soak. *(He eyes her slyly.)* So you was married over there. What, your old man give you the heave-ho?

ROSA *(about to be angry)*. Look . . .

SANDY. Or you leave him? Little Hitler, was he? Hurr. *(A little laugh. A withering look from* ROSA.*)*

No, no offence. *(About to mention 'BERLIN BERTIE'.)* Oh. Fuck. Look, there . . .

But, at once, JOANNE *enters. Her arms are covered up to the elbows in papier mâché. It is on her face and her clothes. She ignores* ROSA *and* SANDY. *She goes to the pile of papers and takes some.* ROSA *watches her with a stony face.* JOANNE *exits.* ROSA *sighs. She stoops down and finds an unopened bottle of Mum champagne. She stares at it. A silence. Then she goes to the box-shaped packet of New Ariel. She picks it up and stares at the champagne and the washing powder in her hands. She weighs one against the other.*

ROSA *(to herself)*. Drunkenness and cleanliness. The power and the fantasy of the West. *(Putting the champagne and washing powder down against the wall. She looks at the boarded up door.)* Why can't I sleep in there?

SANDY. Oh. Yeah.

ROSA. I can't stay at your mum's again, Sandy.

SANDY. Why, she . . .

ROSA. I . . . I can't impose. *(False brightness.)* I mean it would be nice to have a room here tonight, with everyone else. *(A smile.)* And I actually haven't got anywhere else to go.

SANDY. Yeah.

ROSA. So what's in there?

SANDY. Things.

ROSA. What 'things'?

SANDY. I've got onto Alice again and again, I've fucking told her, get the fucking Housing Department in on it . . .

ROSA. 'Things', Sandy?

SANDY. Things what fly about.

ROSA *(horrified)*. You mean the bedroom is infested?

SANDY. It's alright, they don't come out here. For some fucking reason, it's in there they want to be . . .

ROSA. Infested with what?

SANDY. It's alright, they're little,

ROSA *(to herself)*. Oh Alice!

JOANNE enters. She carries a bowl full of set plaster of Paris.

JOANNE. It's gone solid.

ROSA and SANDY look at her. JOANNE turns the bowl over. She has a solid round lump of plaster of Paris in her hand.

It went 'wham'. And was solid. It didn't do that at school. I better start again. *(She puts the lump of plaster of Paris down on the floor and exits.)*

SANDY. If she's pouring that stuff down the sink, we've got more fucking problems.

ROSA. At least she spoke. She didn't speak at all yesterday when we were cleaning. Nor, though it is not my place to criticise, did she lift a finger to help. And this morning she is . . . doing what exactly, with plaster of Paris? Who is she?

SANDY. Goth, in't she.

ROSA. She's a what?

SANDY. A Goth. The black gear and the hair. They got to look suicidal and that, so they look fucking DEEP. That's why they don't speak much.

ROSA. For depth.

SANDY. Load of wankers if you ask me. Still I'll give this to her, she in't one of them WEEKEND GOTHETTES. In the fucking MIDLAND BANK all week, come Friday night into the gear. You can tell a WEEKEND GOTHETTE 'cos they don't dye their hair . . . lose their fucking jobs wouldn't they, pink hair right up the bank manager's nose, too fucking right. Don't they have Goths then, in . . . your East Berlin?

ROSA. They will, any moment now. Right! I must telephone the Housing Department and have the bedroom fumigated. The whole flat, come to that. Is there a number, is there a telephone?

SANDY. Alice threw it out.

ROSA. The number? The 'phone?

SANDY. She er . . . it. Sort of tugged it out the wall and . . . *(A gesture at the door.)* BOP.

ROSA. Why?

SANDY *(with a shrug)*. You know.

ROSA. No I don't.

SANDY. The telly was down to me. *(Bright.)* Here, we going to give the floor a fucking wash, the walls and all . . .

ROSA. What does your caretaker say?

SANDY. My what?

ROSA. Your caretaker, hasn't he reported you to the authorities, for living like this?

SANDY. No. They cut estate caretakers, way back.

ROSA. Who looks after you on the estate then?

SANDY. ?

ROSA *(to herself)*. Oops. Vestiges of socialist thinking in me. *(To SANDY.)* Right I'll go out to a public 'phone and ring, what, the Town Hall?

SANDY. It's Easter. It's the hols. No one'll fucking BE THERE.

ROSA *(to herself)*. England, I'd forgotten what you're like. Everyone free to be alone, and rot away in privacy. *(To SANDY.)* Sorry. I've been away too long.

SANDY. Yeah? *(Awkwardly.)* How long's that then?

ROSA. Fourteen years. Look! Is it usual for Alice to just go off, for a whole night and a day?

SANDY *(he looks at her unable to explain. Then he turns and picks up the bucket and the mop)*. This is tasty, I love it! We can get the carpet down, get a bit of colour in here . . . little vase, nick some flowers out the park . . . yeah, and when we've done we can settle down, stay in, with a bit of a meal . . .

ROSA *is looking at him. He dries up. From here he intermittently mops the floor.*

ROSA. How long have you known my sister?

SANDY. Oh, yonks, we go way back, yeah, Alice and me . . .

ROSA. How long?

SANDY. 'Bout a month.

ROSA. A month.

SANDY. Fucking forever I tell you, the way things go down round here.

ROSA. And you and my sister are lovers?

SANDY. Slags me off all the time, don't she, there in't nothing lovey-dovey about Alice.

ROSA. But you sleep with her?

SANDY. Sort of.

ROSA. 'Sort of', Sandy?

SANDY. Yeah, well it was . . . you know . . . *(An embarrassed gesture.)* I can't talk about this! . . . not with a woman, not with her SISTER . . .

ROSA. Why not?

SANDY. Sex is for blokes in't it, I mean to TALK about, over a few jars and that. I mean, never talk to your mum about sex, would you.

ROSA. Goodness Sandy, you are an interesting fellow.

SANDY. Don't get me going, Rosa, we been getting on famous here, don't go and fucking GET ME GOING, will you . . .

ROSA *(calmly)*. So you sleep with Alice.?

SANDY *(he twice takes a deep breath and breathes out)*. Early on.

ROSA *(keeping still and speaking as quietly as possible)*. Yes.

SANDY. But Alice *(Indistinct.)* . . . into these middleclassy whatnots.

ROSA. Sandy?

SANDY *(loudly)*. Fucking middleclassy whatnots.

ROSA. Yes?

SANDY. Safe sex and that . . . typical fucking social worker, into all the trendy ideas . . . (He flails his arms about. He calms down.) Kept slitting the condom with my thumb nail, didn't I. Safe sex? I'm just no fucking good at it . . . *(He looks sad. He struggles with himself for a moment. Then he shrugs.)* Anyway, now it's just cuddles . . . I mean, the way things is going down these days, cuddles is all you can reasonably expect, in't it . . .

ROSA. Do you love her?

SANDY. What . . . what you putting me through all this FUCKING AGONY for?

ROSA *(angry)*. I'm all the family she's got! And I come back to the country and find her living LIKE THIS. I find you, and some hippy . . .

SANDY. That's not a hippy, that's a Goth . . .

ROSA. I come back to England, desperate to see Alice. And I find a teenage girl and a foul-mouthed layabout, feeding off her.

Where I've been . . . they used to call your kind 'social
parasites'. Are you a parasite, living off my sister?

SANDY. I thought we was getting on . . . parasite, what is this?
What you want to go and say that for? . . . only known you A
FUCKING DAY, but I thought we was friends . . . I thought
we was getting it together, you know, for Alice . . . Getting a bit
of fucking PEACE sorted out down here . . . so what the fuck
you want to go and say I'm a fucking parasite or what?

ROSA. Sandy . . .

SANDY (*whirling around, pulling at the ironing board*). Don't you
SWAN IN HERE and take us lightly, Miss high and mighty
from fuck knows where, don't just SWAN IN . . . (*Knocking the
ironing board about.*) We are doing our best down here . . .
fucking poxy though it be . . .

ROSA. Sandy, don't smash things.

SANDY. You fucking talking to me?

ROSA. You're going to wreck what we've done. It's repetitious
behaviour, it's a pattern . . .

She is irritated with herself. SANDY *is triggered.*

SANDY. Oh! 'PATTERN' is it? I do my best. I pick up this and
that, on the stalls, down the market. I mean I WORK! We're
not nothing down here, you know. No one goes round thinking
they're NOTHING . . . (*His anger escalating.*) Bit of a fucking
PATTERN am I, bit of fucking SCRIBBLE on the walls am I,
just NOTHING, that what I am to you? Bit of FUCKING
GRAFFITI, that what I am? (*He throws the ironing board down.
He whirls round looking for something else to break.*)

ROSA. I apologise. Sandy, just be still and understand, I am
apologising.

A pause. SANDY *still poised.*

England. Green, villages, Shropshire, and London . . . quiet
pubs and mild, mild people taking the dog for a walk, children
playing hopscotch on the pavements, old men in straw hats, old
ladies with big behinds playing bowls in the parks, Londoners
in cloth caps and football scarves . . . that's what I actually saw
in my mind's eye. And my sister there, in a London garden of a
flat in a Victorian terraced house, on a summer evening with
mild, decent friends, all wearing Marks and Spencers' skirts

and sports jackets. My sister, leading a decent life. And back I come . . . to this.

SANDY. Number one, that's England . . . UnBEATable . . . I don't want to know no one who says it's not . . . you don't want to live in the best country in the world, fuck off out of it!

They are staring at each other. Then SANDY deflates. He crouches down. He pulls at the pinafore strings. He pulls the pinafore off and throws it on the floor. A pause. Then ROSA picks the pinafore up and folds it neatly. She puts it in her suitcase.

ROSA. I just want my sister to be safe.

SANDY. Oh YEAH? Right! *(Deflating.)* Right. I know. I know you do. *(They are staring at each other.)* Alice ought to put some time in, being like her sister.

ROSA. Don't fish in deep waters, Sandy. Right! Carpet.

SANDY, *lost in thought.*

Come on don't sit there moping!

SANDY. Oh, yeah.

They lift the carpet, pull off its string and unroll it. SANDY fusses round the edges pulling it straight. They stand back admiring it.

SANDY *(does not look up from the carpet)*. That stain don't matter, does it. I mean, it's not an hole.

JOANNE enters. She carries a large and elaborately ill-made paper and plaster of Paris mask. It is still wet. JOANNE, looking through the mask. ROSA, striking horribly wrong notes.

ROSA. Goodness me!

JOANNE. The eyes is too far apart.

ROSA. It's terrific!

SANDY and JOANNE look at each other. SANDY grimaces.

What's it for?

A pause.

SANDY. There's that carpet shampoo, on the telly. That you froth on, for hoovers.

JOANNE. It's a mask.

SANDY. But we not got an hoover.

ROSA (*to* JOANNE). You just made it for fun?

JOANNE ignores ROSA *but is staring at the crucifix on the wall.*

SANDY (*to* JOANNE). That's hers. All the way from . . .
BERLIN. Berlin.

Nothing from JOANNE. *Then she exits with a 'don't care' flounce.*

ROSA. Oh dear.

SANDY. Don't worry about it.

JOANNE enters again at once. She pauses out of shyness.

JOANNE. There was this man.

SANDY. Oh yeah, I said, didn't I? No I didn't. Oh yeah, that
fucking Kraut.

ROSA looks at them.

JOANNE. He said he wanted you.

SANDY (*to* JOANNE). Said he had Alice's address, didn't he?
(*To* ROSA.) Yeah, sorry, forgot . . . he said he had Alice's
address off of you, he was some Kraut.

ROSA (*she is very still*). What else did he say?

SANDY (*concerned again with the carpet*). Went on about brass
screws, didn't he, right fucking weirdo . . . Maybe we could
turn this over. (*He lifts a corner of the carpet. He grimaces.*) No not
really.

And JOANNE *turns on her heels and exits.*

ROSA (*to herself*). It can't be Joachim. Not sweet suffering . . .

SANDY. Rosa?

ROSA (*she starts. She smiles*). It was my husband.

SANDY. Oh.

ROSA. He's followed me. I'd never have thought it of him. He is
a saint, you see.

SANDY. That guy is?

ROSA's bitterness is odd.

ROSA (*a bitterness*). I am married to the most saintly of men.

SANDY. I'd have thought . . .

ROSA. What?

SANDY. I'd have thought the guy who was here was fucking hard.

ROSA. Oh he has a hard cold centre. *(To herself.)* Saints always do.

SANDY. No, I been round hard men, they've got a mark . . . *(He taps his forehead.)* There, it shines right in your fucking face. I tell you, that Bertie from Berlin, was HARD.

ROSA. Who?

SANDY. That Kraut.

ROSA. What did you say his name was?

SANDY. Bert whatnot. Bert Brick or . . .

ROSA. He said he was 'Bertolt Brecht'?

SANDY. Something like that.

> ROSA *is very frightened.* SANDY's *attention back to the carpet.*

If we cut the stain out and settled for an hole anyway, maybe it wouldn't be that bad. I mean, fucking second-hand anyway, in't it . . .

ROSA. Sandy, the sink.

SANDY. 'Course if we had a chair, a proper chunky chair, we could just plonk it down over it . . . bom bom!

ROSA. Go and look at the sink!

SANDY. You what?

ROSA. Go and see to the sink!

> SANDY, *lost.*

Go and see if that stupid girl has clogged the kitchen sink up with plaster of Paris!

SANDY. Er . . .

ROSA *(to herself)*. Used to play that game, Alice. When you were tiny, I'd give you a bath at bedtime. A bubble in the bath. It goes down the drainpipe. Underground, the manhole in the garden. The river. The sea. The bubble round the world. Why would HE come here? He has no REASON to come here. *(A thought hits her.)* Oh dear God, no . . . *(To SANDY.)* Go and see if she's clogged up the whole world with that stuff!

SANDY. Alright! *(A pause.)* I will.

He shrugs and exits. ROSA still. A pause. Then she goes to her suitcase. She pulls at the contents. She finds a grey paper file. She is extremely distressed. She looks around the room. She goes to the corner and puts it into the mess there, pulling things on top of it. She backs away. She is at the centre of the carpet. She kneels and prays. She does not hold her hands together.

The Lord is my shepherd . . . *(And to the audience -)* The night of the seventh of October, 1989.

And at once –

2.

Flashback. The light is tight around the edge of the carpet. ROSA is kneeling in prayer in a small, ill-lit room. She does not hold her hands together.

ROSA. The Lord is my shepherd, I shall not want. He maketh me to lie down in green pastures: he leadeth me beside the still waters. *(To herself.)* Thank God we never had children, in this vile city, this vile, vile, vile . . . *(And continues to pray.)*
He restoreth my soul: he leadeth me in the paths of righteousness for his name's sake. *(To herself.)* Name sake, name sick . . . *(And continues to pray.)*
Yea, though I walk through the valley of the shadow of death, I will fear no evil: for thou art with me; thy rod and thy staff they comfort me.
Thou preparest a table before me in the presence of mine enemies: thou anointest my head with oil; my cup runneth over. *(To herself.)* Are they being beaten in the police vans with the little wired-over windows, vile wired windows . . . *(And continues to pray.)*
Surely goodness and mercy shall follow me all the days of my life: and I will dwell in the house of the Lord forever.
She remains still. She does not cross herself. A doorbell rings. She glances to one side. The doorbell rings again. She sucks a breath in. The doorbell rings again. At once she stands and exits running. The stage is empty. A pause. 'BERTIE' enters. He is not in the suit of Act One. He wears worn light-blue jeans, scuffed white trainers, a grey open-necked shirt and

a tracksuit top. A stain of blood runs down the front of his clothing. He carries a plastic shopping bag.

NB: the actor has picked up the champagne bottle and the packet of New Ariel. They are in the bag. He puts the shopping bag down. He stands legs astride. He is out of breath. He leans forward, hands on his hips. Then he does a quick exercise several times, left hand touching right toes, right hand touching left toes. He straightens. His breath is controlled. ROSA re-enters. She stands watching him, hugging herself. A pause.

'BERTIE'. Waren Sie heute Nacht auf der Strasse? Waren Sie Teilnehmer an der Demonstration? *(And from here, no accent. The pretence is that the scene is in German.)* Were you on the streets tonight? Were you taking part in the demonstrations? *(He takes out an identification card.)* Ministry for State Security. *(He puts the card away).* Well, bitch? Were you out, running with the rest of them, the pack, on heat? Shouting 'democracy', 'New Forum' ... with all the other scum?'

ROSA *(to herself)*. My turn has come.

'BERTIE'. Where's your husband? The holy man, your pastor husband.

She cannot speak for fear.

Is he hiding here, behind his wife's skirt? Or is he being brave out on the streets? Or perhaps he is in his church, on his knees, praying? We could have him on his knees in another place tonight you know, on all fours, with something hot up his arse. Do you want to join him?

ROSA. Not here.

'BERTIE'. What, bitch?

ROSA. He's not here! *(She tries to collect herself.)* I was working late tonight. This is my office ... Joachim doesn't come here much. I see my patients here, I'm a psychiatrist ...

'BERTIE' *(very nastily)*. Don't be stupid, I know what your so-called profession is. I know everything about you. Your file is as long as a Dostoevsky novel, and as appalling a read.

'BERTIE' *is impassive.* ROSA, *trying to keep it together. A pause.*

ROSA. Yes, it's my office, I use it. On my own. It's my space, for me, that's what we agreed between us, he has his work, I have mine, I'm married to a wonderful man, a busy man ...

'BERTIE' *(interrupting her).* You are married to a man who has indulged in activities hostile to the state for twenty years.

ROSA. I cannot talk about my husband . . .

'BERTIE'. Married in the West, didn't you? Then in 1975, came with him to the East. 'I am with my suffering flock', is that not what he said in his first sermon here? 'Suffering flock'. Either the remark of a saint, or of a sanctimonious idiot.

ROSA. I cannot talk about my husband.

'BERTIE'. Or just a very . . . naive . . . man. A great lighter of candles, much given to the incantation of prayers for peace and democracy, a great keeper of vigils for all kinds of social malcontents in his church. 'Rosa', an English rose, why did you give yourself to such a clown? *(He laughs.)* You must be one of the few people who crossed the Berlin Wall, going the wrong way. *(Wearily.)* Or, as we call it, the people's anti-fascist security wall. (ROSA, *trying not to weep. A pause.)*

ROSA. I was here working late tonight, that's all . . . I'm not ready! *(She tries to laugh.)* A Stasi man calls. We've talked about what we would do when it happened. We've prayed. We have told ourselves 'we are ready'. But I'm not, not . . .

'BERTIE'. Surely a psychiatrist has some element of self-control . . . reserves of self-knowledge that are denied to the rest of us? Be assured, you and your pastor Joachim could have been arrested at any time. We have played such a GAME, over the years, with your husband. Did he really believe that he was actually hiding criminals from The Ministry of State Security, from US, the 'sword and shield of the party'? Did he really think we didn't know who was crammed into the crypt of his church, even at times in the attic of your manse across the street? His little flock of social deviants on the run, the odd Christian democrat, crazy Baptist or Zionist, the occasional bad poet.

ROSA. You're not here to arrest me.

'BERTIE'. I did not say that. *(A pause. And with sudden brightness.)* Well! I've been up since five-thirty. Big day, long day, Founders' Day. The German Democratic Republic is forty years old today. The birthday of socialism in our country, what a lovely day. Big parade. Big speeches. Did you hear the broadcast of comrade Erich Honecker's call for world peace? Isn't the future bright for our Republic? What do you say?

*She tries to speak but cannot. 'BERTIE' wipes his forehead and his face
with his hand.*

Something for you.

*He goes to the neck of the shopping bag. ROSA flinches. But he takes
out a packet of New Ariel washing powder and a bottle of Mum
champagne. He places them carefully on the carpet. She stares at them.*

Look. *(He rips open the pack of New Ariel.)* With New Ariel Ultra,
you can use just half your usual amount. And, look! *(He points
to a logo on the packet.)* Ariel Ultra is working towards a better
environment. And is approved by the Worldwide Fund For
Nature. But what's new with Ariel Ultra is this! *(He takes out a
plastic ball).* The Arielator! With the scoop . . . *(He takes out the
spoon-like scoop.)* . . . you load Ariel Ultra into the Arielator and
place it, upwards, on top of your laundry. No need to prewash,
just select your mainwash programme. Then the Arielator can
be used over and over again, without any risk to your laundry.
Is that not a wonder of the world?

ROSA *(a pause).* I . . . I don't have a washing machine.

'BERTIE' *(a feigned surprise).* No? Aren't you a party member?

ROSA. Humil . . .

'BERTIE'. What?

ROSA. Humil . . .

'BERTIE'. What?

ROSA. Are you trying to humiliate me?

'BERTIE'. I've brought you gifts. Champagne and washing
powder, the frankincense and myrrh of the Western world.
From a special party shop, hidden but actually just round the
corner, open twenty-four hours a day if you've got the right
card, and a Ministry of State Security card is VERY right.
YOU STUPID FUCKING COW of course I'm not here to
arrest you. *(A pause.)* I'm here to confess. *(A pause.)* I want to
confess my sins.

ROSA *is frozen.*

Isn't that what you do to a Christian? And you are a Christian
AND a trained psychiatrist. I mean, darling, you are just what
I need tonight.

ROSA *finds her legs have gone. She plumps down on the carpet.*

Help me.

ROSA. How can . . . *(She controls herself. She looks at the bloodstains on his clothing.)* Why are you . . .

'BERTIE'. Oh!

He pulls at his shirt to look at it. The movement is like a child who has messed his clothing.

A television crew from the West. They were to film the Founders' Day ceremony, instead they were filming the demonstrations. I beat up the cameraman. Got the bastard into a courtyard, gave him a good going over. That's one lackey of the capitalist media who won't forget the death of socialism in a hurry.

ROSA *takes this in. Then low.*

ROSA. How can I possibly help you?

'BERTIE'. Be a psychiatrist! *(He laughs sarcastically.)* Identify the . . . traumas? The personality disorders? The complexes that threaten my . . . what is the bourgeois jargon? . . .My 'interaction with the real world?' Help me. HEAL me. *(Low.)* Be cool water. Lay cool hands on my burning brow. Heal my mind.

ROSA *is breathing too quickly. She steadies herself.*

ROSA. The relationship between a therapist and a patient is one of mutual trust. On neutral ground. How can I trust you? What is 'neutral' about tonight, when you are a threat to my very life?

'BERTIE' *pauses. Then he takes out a snub-barrelled pistol that was tucked in the waist of his jeans. He holds it in his hand. They both look at it.*

'BERTIE'. At first we were instructed to go on the streets tonight, armed. The Felix Dzierzynski Guard Regiment were to be deployed, all over the city.

ROSA *(she is shocked)*. The . . .

'BERTIE'. What? So ignorant of the institutions of your adopted country?

ROSA. I know who the Felix Dzierzynski Guards are. Stasi crack troops, were to be sent against unarmed people, in the streets of East Berlin?

'BERTIE'. By the order of comrade Erich Honecker, personally. We were to have a massacre, once and for all. If socialism is to die in Germany, it should have an unforgettable funeral, in good Prussian style, yes? That's what we were telling ourselves this morning! We would make the efforts of the Chinese in Tiananmen Square look like a squabble in a kindergarten playground. But at noon, the order was countermanded. We were to crack a few heads, but nothing decisive, nothing CLEANSING, nothing . . . cathartic? *(He pauses.)* A few of us took weapons, as a gesture. To what might have been.

ROSA. Who . . . countermanded the order?

'BERTIE' *(looks at her. He grins)*. The KGB. *(Laughter. It dies. Then bitterly.)* Our fraternal comrades from Moscow, from the heartland, the bulwark of the socialist camp, the well-head of the hopes of the oppressed peoples of the world, the source of our strength. The KGB insisted the order was cancelled. *(He puts the pistol down on the carpet beside the New Ariel and the champagne.)* You've won.

ROSA. Nothing . . . The Central Committee is still in power. The wall is closed. No doubt the lights are still burning in the Stasi buildings on the Frankfurter Allee. . . . Nothing's been won.

'BERTIE'. Believe me, from tonight, you have won. The buildings, the institutions of the state, the Party itself, even the wall . . . are phantoms now. Dust, suspended in the air. It will take just a breath . . . *(A gesture of blowing a feather from the palm of his hand.)*

ROSA. No.

'BERTIE'. Hunh! *(A pause.)* You will have to do without the habit of being watched. It had not occurred to me, on the way here . . . In the months, the years ahead, you will be as lost as I.

ROSA. No . . .

'BERTIE'. Come! Tell me, as a student of psychology, don't you and I have a shared dependency? *(Leaning close to her.)* Pastor's wife, dissident heroine, hasn't it begun to gnaw at you? An absence, in the very soul. A terrible grief for something that is dying, minute by minute as we talk in this room . . . and will leave us, alone. Useless. Weak. Hollow. Has not our state created a dependency, even in those who rejected it? What will I do without the Party, the Ministry? *(He grins.)* And what will you do, without the fear? *(Suddenly jaunty.)* I know all about fear, my life too has been watched over. 'The Firm' looks after its own . . . 'The Firm'. That is what we call ourselves.

ROSA. You mean even secret policemen will have their own sense of humour?

'BERTIE' *(icily)*. No not really.

A pause.

ROSA. I . . . don't know your name.

'BERTIE'. We never give our names do we, in a conversation such as this. Never give your real name, never meet again. How long will THAT habit last? *(A pause.)* Shall we say 'Bertolt Brecht'?

ROSA. Why not? *(Finally able to collect herself.)* Why do you come to me, like this?

'BERTIE'. I told you.

ROSA. To be healed? I can't do that.

'BERTIE'. Why not?

ROSA. Can't you see I think ANYTHING you say is hopelessly twisted with lies?

'BERTIE' *(he shrugs)*. You must have a technique for dealing with compulsive liars. *(He grins.)* Use it on me.

ROSA. Everything you say . . . I think it's torture. To destroy me. To get something from me.

'BERTIE'. Why think that? We are just a man and a woman in a room.

ROSA. That's ridiculous.

'BERTIE'. Why? Surely you, the Christian healer, have a faith in salvation, that the worst dog can turn? Aren't we free to reinvent ourselves?

ROSA. No. I'm very frightened but I tell you, professionally, I don't accept you as my patient. Maybe you're going to hurt me . . . But I choose not to treat you. You force yourself on me. I won't tolerate it . . . I won't have my profession as a doctor, which I value very much, distorted and besmirched, by whatever sick game you want to play.

BERTIE *(he scoffs)*. Hunh!

ROSA. Anything I say to you is to get you to leave this room, and never appear in my life again. The good faith of patient and doctor is impossible between us.

'BERTIE'. In this 'new era' that is being born about us, will there be any conversations 'in good faith'? The grand world views are collapsing into rubble – what will there be between us that we can rely on? All relationships will be tainted now . . . *(He laughs.)* Come come, Madam psychiatrist . . . as an experiment, under these historically unique conditions, aren't you tempted to work me over? Don't you even want to know what my job is in the Ministry?

ROSA *looks away.*

A pause.

ROSA *(dragging the question out of herself).* What is your job in the Ministry?

'BERTIE'. Was my job, after tonight. *(He eyes her.)* I am responsible for quality control. Of the products of the Engineering Special Device Construction Factory.

ROSA, *blank.*

It is just off the Lenin-Allee. You may have noticed a wall, three metres high? Ask one of the locals for 'the secret Stasi factory'. They will not point it out to you, but they will know what you mean.

ROSA. What do you . . . make at this factory?

'BERTIE' *(irritably).* The listening devices! The recorders, the microphones, the 'BUGS' of course! I have to check their efficiency in the field . . . *(Turning away, as if irritated with himself.)* . . . Sensitive work, which is why I am a political officer, of an intimidatingly high rank . . . *(Then turning on* ROSA.*)* If capitalism is to triumph, perhaps the factory can make hearing aids, for the deaf? The 'market' will be wide open for a product of the quality we can guarantee. The deaf will be able to hear what everyone is saying within a radius of three miles, eh? *(And angrily.)* You stupid, doe-eyed, ignorant woman, with your phoney, holier-than-thou Sunday school . . . come-on, so PRISSY, adjusting your little plastic halo from Jesus . . . I monitored the microphones in your home! Regularly! I have heard you cook in your kitchen, shit in your toilet, fuck in your bedroom. He likes you doggy style, doesn't he, the good Pastor

Joachim? Likes you from behind. And on really tender nights, he asks to put himself in your mouth, a 'special' for Lent, eh? Raunchy nights at the manse! The lads used to love them, listening from the house just across the way.

ROSA *(low)*. The Lord is my . . .

'BERTIE' *(close to her)*. And there have been rows between you in the last few months. Terrible rows.

ROSA *(low)*. The Lord is my . . .

'BERTIE'. Just as victory is in sight for your husband's friends . . . the oppositionists, the dreamers, the anti-communists, THE GOOD who will be heroes in the new German history books, you have come to hate them . . .

ROSA *(low)*. The Lord is my . . .

'BERTIE'. You've given your life for those people, with their shining eyes and bad breath, the stink of the hunted on their skin. Now, when they meet in your living room, to plot for the last days of socialism, you are overwhelmed with a physical repulsion. And you begin to suspect them. Suspect them, morally, intellectually.

ROSA. No!

'BERTIE'. Don't deny it! I have heard you shouting these things at your husband!

ROSA. There are the pure in heart, though you can't know what that means. That is lost on a man like you.

'BERTIE'. The 'pure in heart' will never have any influence in the re-united Germany. *(To himself.)* If that is what we are to suffer. *(He pauses.)* But the others, who have crouched in your crypt and in your attic? You begin to see they are not what they say they are. Not democrats at all. Suddenly, you fear that you have harboured fanatics, as bad as we whom they have sought so long to replace? There is even one, who acts as the most religious but whose mask is beginning to slip? Who has friends in the Republican Party in West Germany? *(Low.)* A neo-Nazi? A Hitlerite, Rosa, in your loft?

ROSA. Victims are victims! You can't pick and choose amongst the oppressed, you can't decide only to help those you like!

'BERTIE'. That's what Joachim says but YOU DISAGREE, DON'T YOU!

ROSA. We always knew you were there. When we talked, when we touched, at . . . the most secret moments . . . we knew our lives were naked . . . before your microphones, your camera lenses. But we lived. And all the recordings you have, and the photographs and the transcripts and the reports of spies, they tell you . . . nothing. You may have every little detail about our lives, but you KNOW nothing about what we are. You've no idea about the Christian life. No idea what it's like to bear . . . *(She stutters.)* W . . . w . . . witness to Christ's love, to seek redemption, in His love. You've no idea what it means to say 'I am crossed out in Christ.' And be reborn.

'BERTIE'. What shit. THAT is an ideology? Did you know syphilis appeared on the planet, the same time that Christianity began? Both have merrily rotted minds for two millennia. *(Low.)* But you are very brave.

ROSA, *controlling breathlessness. She almost asks a question. He seizes on that.*

'BERTIE'. Ah! What?

ROSA. No.

'BERTIE'. What, what?

ROSA. How could you ever come to this?

'BERTIE' *(softly)*. Ah.

ROSA. How can anyone become a part of such a terrible thing? Did you believe in it?

'BERTIE'. I never had to ask myself that question.

ROSA. I don't understand it.

'BERTIE' *(irritably)*. I never had to believe 'it', I was 'it'. *(He laughs.)* A sense of power can sustain you, though many things you know, and I had power. I could fuck anyone I passed in the street, anyone. No, I can't say 'I have lost my faith.'

(A pause.) As you have lost yours. *(He grins again.)* That I do know about you, from the microphones.

ROSA'*s hands tremble. He scoffs.*

'Crossed out in Christ.' *(And close to her.)* Are you a deserter too?

ROSA *shakes her head abruptly.*

Where will you go, to your sister in London? She wrote to you a lot.

ROSA *(low, exhausted).* Will I ever feel . . . the hands of you people . . . lifted from my life?

'BERTIE' *(low, spreading his hands before her).* I am disappearing. Look. You can see through me. I'm a ghost, I can't touch anything. I'm slipping away, through the walls, into the air. Huh? *(And brightly.)* And there's a big world, a big world. Saudi Arabia has already made discrete inquiries amongst my comrades. They are interested in employing instructors of certain techniques, you understand. The salaries are spectacular. *(Low again.)* I do confess my sins to you. I do, sincerely. I want to prove my 'good faith'. *(He pulls the shopping bag toward him. He takes out a file. He puts his hand over her mouth. He gives her the file. He shakes his head with his finger to his lips. She looks about her. He picks up the gun and tucks it into the belt of his jeans.)*

'BERTIE'. So, you refuse me treatment?

She is silent.

I am not fit for salvation?

ROSA. No. You are not.

'BERTIE'. Ha! No Christian whose belief is intact could say that! No matter. *(He picks up the champagne bottle. He is opening it.)* I will have to crawl sideways through life, with this cracked psyche of mine, eh? Yes yes, of course your office is microphoned. If the recorders are still turning in the Frankfurter Allee, I have made a most effective confession. I do believe I have changed my life. Thank you. *(A Prussian click of his heels.)* Though I think it would be unwise to turn up to work tomorrow. *(He smiles.)* I am 'reborn'.

He pops the champagne cork. He swigs from the bottle. He wipes the froth from himself. He puts the bottle down before her and leans across her. He kisses her on the mouth. She does not move nor withdraw. He picks up the shopping bag and goes. A silence. ROSA is still. Then she opens the file. She reads a little. Turns a page. Turns another. She panics. She picks up the file.

ROSA. Hide. Hide. Hide.

Repeating 'hide' she runs out of the light. She returns without the file. She kneels before the packet of New Ariel and the champagne. She is silent. Then she grabs the packet of New Ariel and pours its contents out. She grabs the bottle and pours champagne upon the soap powder. Flashback ends. A return to the light of the London flat.

3.

ROSA, *pouring the champagne on to the washing powder.* ALICE *stands in the doorway. She looks dirty and exhausted. She carries the day's newspapers under her arm. She is staring at the kneeling* ROSA.

ALICE. Don't YOU go potty. If YOU go potty, I don't know what I'll do.

Change –

Aside No. 2 'The Secret Jesus'

> ROSA.

I want to go
    Over the sea
        to Palestine
Where the tomb
    of Jesus lies
        Secret and empty
In the cool of the night

I want to know
    The silence wherein
        He lay, the silence
That stills the soul

I want to be
    laid on the cold slab
        of His grave
Naked with Him
    my sweet Lord
the secret Jesus of heresy

Sh! Sh!
    the woman's heresy
        whispered by girls
In the convent school
By novices
    in dark corridors

Locked in their nunnery

A pause.

For I am the lover of my Lord
In the tomb
He comes to life his lips to mine
He moves inside my womb
He moans, He comes to life
In my arms
I pin Him to my body's cross
I nail, I torture
I am His wife
And I am murdering Him
He passes into me
And dies again
I lick the sweat from His cooling skin
I roll back the stone
And stand in the garden
Blazing, wild
In the glory of my sin
To appear to the women waiting there
Bitch mother Mary
Martha hausfrau
Magdalene the tart
Who was always after him and shout
'He is not here
He rose IN ME and now he's dead
And I am pregnant with his child
I am the resurrection and the life
Not He.'

Change: the scene is restored.
ALICE, *exactly as before.*

ALICE. Don't YOU go potty. If YOU go potty, I don't know
what I'll do. *(She sags. The newspapers slip to the floor. A blackout.)*

Interval.

ACT THREE

Easter Sunday, April 15th, 1990.

Evening in the flat. It is dark. The lamps are switched on. Because some of the lamps are shaded and some are not, the light in the room is both garish and patchy. The champagne bottle has been moved but the mess of Ariel powder remains. The lump of set plaster of Paris is where JOANNE *left it. The Sunday newspapers both tabloid and broadsheet are spread out on the carpet.*

1.

ALICE *is curled up on one of the mattresses beneath blankets. The bowl that was used for plaster of Paris is by her head.* ROSA *is sitting on a rolled up mattress.* JOANNE *is in a handstand against a wall.* ALICE *is counting the seconds of* JOANNE'*s handstand under her breath. A long pause.* ROSA *becomes increasingly restless as the pause progresses. Then –*

ROSA. I've got to stay here tonight.

ALICE. Sh! *(She continues to count.)*

ROSA. Two nights at Sandy's mother's. I've never experienced TALK like that before.

ALICE. Sh! *(She continues to count.)*

ROSA. Everything she'd do, she'd describe. 'I'm putting a kettle on now, for you and me' . . . then the memory . . . 'Sandy's dad the bastard was a funny one for tea' . . . then the tea bag, and the nostalgia, for other tea bags, hundreds of tea bags, back down the years . . . Why? Is it conversation to repel people? Words, used to make others back away, language as bad breath . . .

ALICE. You're the psychiatrist, you tell me.

ROSA. I don't know. There's a whole difference between treating people and experiencing them. *(A pause.)* Oh God I want to smoke. Why did I give up smoking?

ALICE. Sh! Five hundred and forty-eight . . .

ROSA *(looking at her watch)*. Let me time her.

ALICE. Fortynine . . .

ROSA. What's happened to your watch? You had mother's watch.

ALICE. Oh shut up sister!

And she concentrates on JOANNE. *A pause.*

ROSA. It wasn't health. I gave up smoking when I was
converted. When I think of myself then . . . *(She laughs.)* Giving
up smoking was a penance. I dedicated all the fags of the future
to Jesus. I wanted to go forth into the world shining, with a
fresh UPWARD look on my face. You used to see that look on
East German television. At sports meetings. Athletes, holding
up flaming torches, looking upward and shining. *(To* ALICE.*)* I
envy it, you know. I wish I could still . . . look upward, and
shine.

ALICE. Oh for . . . *(And scrabbles amongst the blankets. She finds a
packet of cigarettes and a box of matches. She throws them at* ROSA.
She continues to count.)

ALICE. If you want to smoke, smoke.

SANDY *enters.*

SANDY. You sure this geezer's going to show? I'm going round
and round, I can't see the fucker nowhere.

ALICE. You are our very own PRIVATE DICK and bodyguard,
isn't he Rosa, where was I?

ROSA. Five hundred and eighty.

SANDY *(looking at the newspapers)*. You're not going to fucking
CRUD the place up again, are you? And anyway, what if I do
go and catch this Kraut, sniffing round the estate? What the
fuck do I do then? Bop him one?

ALICE. Look to your 'hard' friends. Aren't 'the lads' out there
too, running through the night? Scouring the streets on our
behalf?

SANDY. Nah they got pissed off. Down the pub in't they. Where
the fuck I should be and all . . .

ROSA. If you see him . . . *(Low.)* Just come and tell us.

ALICE. Protect us. With your mighty Magnum arms.

SANDY. Oh. *(Uncertain.)* Right then. *(Going. But he turns back.)* 'Course you're not going to tell me who this Kraut is, are you, no WAY are you going to tell me what this is all about, the fuck no. (ROSA *and* ALICE *trying not to smirk.*)

ALICE. It concerns recent geopolitical and historical events, Sandy, which have triggered a deep psychological trauma, afflicting a member of my family. *(With a grimace at* ROSA.) And with which I am entwined.

A pause.

SANDY. Oh fuck it. *(He exits quickly.* ALICE *and* ROSA *look at each other. They grin.*)

ROSA. Sandy's sweet. *(Unsure.)* In his way. I did my thesis on compulsive swearing.

ALICE. He's good for cuddles. Some of us do need the odd cuddle, you know. A bit of fur, some SMELLY HEAT now and then. We are not all blessed with total self control.

ROSA *(she is offended)*. Really? Is that how you see me? 'Blessed' with total self control?

ALICE. Aren't you? . . . eighty . . . five hundred and what? YES YOU ARE, say ninety-one, five hundred and ninety-two . . . And preachy.

ROSA. Preachy. I see.

ALICE *(sullen)*. Messing things up with curtains and carpets. I mean what are you doing here, big sister?

ROSA. I've got nowhere to live.

ALICE *(low)*. Rosa, don't let's have the big Brine sisters' row, like of old, please, I couldn't bear it. *(About to move to comfort her.)*

ROSA. No. *(Repelling her.)* I don't call doing SOMETHING about the filth in here, 'messing things up'.

ALICE. It's not about cleaning things up, it's a way of getting at me, of preaching at me. And, oh gawd, of getting at yourself. SOD it Rosa. That awful family gene we have, the MORAL SELF-SCRUTINY gene.

ROSA. And you, of course, are the last person in the world who needs MORAL SELF SCRUTINY . . .

ALICE. Too right.

ROSA. Then why are you taking drugs?

Both of them are shocked at the direct question that is suddenly between them. A pause.

ALICE. DON'T . . . YOU . . . DARE.

ROSA. Why are you doing it?

ALICE. DON'T DARE.

ROSA. I know the signs. It's running you ragged . . .

ALICE. DON'T . . .

ROSA. . . . You were gone a whole night. Then you came back, yesterday. And went to sleep on a mattress. And woke up, what mid-afternoon today? Woke up and threw up your insides.

ALICE. That tone, that tone of old, my skin is crawling.

ROSA. You won't have any skin left.

ALICE. Nowhere to live? You want shelter, why, are you DAMAGED, sister? I mean, what's YOUR trouble? WHY have you limped back to England? . . . Did this Berlin Bertie fuck you?

ROSA is irritated at ALICE's diversion.

Did you fall in love with him, become his mistress, meet in East Berlin flats, handcuffs, leather, 'bondage with Stasi man'? I mean, did you go all the way down to hell, sister? 'Bondage with Stasi man? Maybe that's all that's going to be left of the great communist experiment, the attempt to remake humanity . . . a few pornographic fantasies. And what about Joachim? I couldn't stand Joachim. Those little blue eyes, that wispy hair. Did he join in? Did you all go down together?

ALICE is breathless.

ROSA. Reading the letters you sent, I prided myself, I said 'Alice is well, living in a free country, and a progressive young woman.'

ALICE. I am! I am light years ahead.

ROSA. Alice, the risk. You'll flay yourself alive. I've got to say something.

ALICE, a sudden movement withdrawing and hunching up pulling the blanket to her.

ALICE. Say I'm grieving for the end of the cold war. I'm not FRIGHTENED enough anymore . . .

ROSA. *(low)*. For Heaven's sake . . .

ALICE. Say I want my own personal bomb . . . Great! SAY anything at all, BUT DON'T SAY IT TO ME. There's no WHY, we do what we do do, do, or, do what we do . . .

ROSA. Prided myself, 'My young sister back in England is a progressive young woman.'

ALICE. And I am! I am light years ahead.

ROSA. That's not you talking, you see.

ALICE. How do you know what's me, or, what's not, or, you've not been here! You've been fighting Marxism-Leninism for Christ!

ROSA. Don't you feel anything for yourself?

In a rage of frustration ALICE *hits the blankets four times with her fist. Then she is still. A pause.*

ALICE. *(low)*. I don't have to feel anything 'cos I know I am excrement . . . alright? Happy? *(And she snaps out of it.)* Gawd . . . *(Nodding through the count.)* five hundred and ninety-nine . . . six hundred . . . *(To* JOANNE.) You're there!

JOANNE *continues to handstand. The tension between* ALICE *and* ROSA *snaps. They smirk.*

ROSA. We blame all this on our mother, don't we.

ALICE. Oh shut up sister. *(To* JOANNE.) Joanne! Six hundred! You've broken your own record. You can come out of it now. Joanne!

JOANNE *remains dead still and upside down.* ROSA *and* ALICE, *looking at her.*

ROSA. Why does she want to be upside down?

ALICE. She's in training.

ROSA. What for, a visit to Australia?

ALICE. For death.

ROSA *(nods)*. A visit to Australia.

ALICE. Joanne is a mime 'artiste'. She is preparing for a

European tour. Her performance depicts the end of the world.

ROSA. I see.

ALICE. DON'T say what does she know about death to take it to
Europe, what does she know about Europe, even.

ROSA. Alright I won't.

ALICE. Don't say what RIGHT has she got to put a funny hat
down on the ground, under the Brandenburg Gate, and bum a
few marks off passers-by by waving her arms about pretending
to be a nuclear mushroom cloud . . .

ROSA. Alright.

ALICE. DON'T SAY what right has this kid got, with a nose . . .
clown's nose on a rubber band over her face, to thumb a lift,
from a lorry driver with a load of Euro lamb, by the turn off to
Belsen Belsen . . .

ROSA. Right.

ALICE. DON'T SAY doesn't she know she's flitting through
RUBBLE, don't say doesn't she know she's being arty, across a
continent that's . . . that's a tacky, built-up area, McDonald's
and holiday homes over a SMASHED-UP GRAVEYARD,
don't say doesn't she realise her stupid little mime . . . is an
insult to millions who have suffered all too recently, yourself
included, in your way, sister mine, DON'T SAY IT, or,
because, or, I can't bear it and I think I'm not going to be sick
again. *(She leans to the bowl.)* Yeah, I'm not going to be sick
again.

ROSA. What's happened, Alice? Just tell.

And at once JOANNE *does a backward roll out of her handstand to sit
cross-legged before them.* JOANNE *stares, they stare back.*

Change –

Aside No. 3. 'Human Flight'

JOANNE.

I think we could do it
            I think
We could fly

Just get RIGHT

your feet, your body
RIGHT and twist

Turn a strange corner
arch your back
And SLIP in through

Open a door in the air
free
Human flight

It's in us
I know
It's a KNACK

All you've got to do
is just
Slip through

Be great for bloody busking
that!
The all-time greatest act.

Change: the scene is restored.

ROSA. Just tell.

JOANNE *turns her back on them and adopts a lotus flower position.*

ALICE. He BIT her fifty-seven times.

ROSA. I'm sorry?

ALICE. Baby Kylie's father. Fifty-seven human bites were on the baby's body. *(A pause.)* He'd bitten her, fifty-seven times, to revive her.

A pause.

ALICE. After he'd sort-of THWACKED her, against the wall, holding the baby's ankles, like beating a carpet . . .

A pause.

ALICE. With a carpet-beater, or a double-handed tennis backhand . . .

ROSA. YES! *(A pause.)* Go on.

ALICE. But don't you see? Baby Kylie's mum and dad, they'd got angry with her, when she'd got burnt, burnt by the double-barred electric fire! Which the father had put her on, or. He'd put their ten-month baby on . . .

A silence. They look at each other.

They left Kylie outside Casualty, at King's, in the middle of the night. Already dead, but well wrapped up. And with a soft toy, a kind of fluffy penguin.

ROSA. I . . .

ALICE. There weren't any dents in the wall. The police found they'd been filled in with Polyfilla, and painted over. The police LOVED the polyfilled dents, lots of measurements, lots of photographs. The mother had done them, Demetra Arthur, mother of baby Cindy Arthur.

ROSA. I can't . . .

ALICE. Nor can I.

ROSA. Imagine . . .

ALICE. No.

ROSA. What in the name of . . . *(A pause.)* And . . .

ALICE. Yes I was the social worker. I 'deemed the blood-tie to the child's mother to be all important'. I thought Demetra could handle it. I really thought I'd got through to her, I . . . *(She pauses.)* If I could keep her away from Sylvester.

A blank look from ROSA.

Baby Kylie's father. And the Council had 'A Good Practice Guide' . . . bless it's worn-out, all-in-holes red socks . . . We were to do all we could to keep black families together. Quote – 'Provide the child with SURVIVAL SKILLS necessary for living in a racist society'. Gawd, what survival skills do you need, when you're nine months old and your daddy, I . . . *(She pauses.)* There's a black bitch on the council who said it was all my fault, middle-class whitey social worker does not understand black CULTURE . . . I mean, I don't know, this BLOKE burnt his baby on an electric fire, beat her head against the wall then bit her to wake her up when she was dead . . . I mean, what's this to do with CULTURE? To do with RACE, to do with anything, this is just FUCKING HUMANITY getting on with daily life . . ., or. The kid was under an interim court order, eleven days after she was born . . . Her father . . .

ROSA. Sylvester?

ALICE *(stares at her for a moment, then continues).* . . . been convicted
for causing brain damage to baby Kylie's brother, aged three,
and done two years . . . but, with the new baby, hope? Eternal?
For SOMEONE. I argued, let baby Kylie live with her mum,
'long as Demetra went to stay with the kid's grandma . . .
which was OK for a couple of months, BUT then the grandma
had the electricity to her flat cut off and . . .

ROSA. Demetra went back to Sylvester. *(A pause.)* And she looked
on, as he killed the child?

ALICE. Why did she fill up the holes in the wall . . . I really can't
. . . understand.

ROSA. No? I can. Fear can do wonderfully strange things. *(But
ALICE is looking aside with her mouth open, as if something has caught
her eye. A pause. And out of it.)* So you didn't know Demetra had
gone back to the pig of a husband.

ALICE *says nothing.*

Oh Alice. You didn't check. You didn't go round to see if
Demetra and the baby were still with the grandmother.

ALICE, *a little shake of the head.*

ALICE *(a pause).* I had a cold.

ROSA. A cold.

ALICE. That's all.

ROSA *(trying to convince herself).* You were run down. You should
have gone sick, you didn't, you . . .

ALICE. I said, I had a cold! You know, train drivers, social
workers, we're not allowed to make a simple mistake. For good
reason, people die. *(Change. Sing-song.)* And now I am
suspended. On full pay. Waiting for Sedgrove. The re-port of
an indie – indie – indePENdent enquiry, headed by a QC. And
I am waiting. For all the terrible things to be said about the
baby, the tabloids going on about the parents being black, and
activists on the left going on about me . . . *(Very distressed.)* Me,
me, that I'm incompetent, that I don't care, that I'm a racist,
white slag . . .

ROSA. How long has this been hanging over you?

ALICE *(irritated).* Two years.

ROSA. And all that time you were writing to me about your

wonderful life.

ALICE. But you were fighting the evil communists for Jesus. How could my 'trouble' be the equal to your suffering, sister dear? What had I, in the West, to whinge about? We've got democracy here, we've got the FREE MARKET in bashed baby's heads . . .

ROSA. That is desperately silly.

A silence. They are both very upset. They compose themselves.

ALICE. Come on then, come on. Blame me.

ROSA. My dear . . . *(A movement towards her.)*

ALICE *(to repel her)*. No. No.

A silence, as they look at each other.

ROSA. You're not to blame, Alice.

ALICE. 'Course I am. And if you dare use religious language . . . 'taking on the sins of the world' or some such . . . I will seriously vomit serious vomit, right?

ROSA. Oh right.

ALICE *(she lights up)*. Aren't we fabulous? The fabulous Brine sisters. No? Look at us!

ROSA *(low)*. I don't want to look at us at this moment, Alice, really, I don't . . .

ALICE. Me, or, evil social worker, a witch of our time, BIG STORY, dead baby, villainess of the right. Fiend. But you? A Darling of the new World Order! Dissident from the East, yum yummy, a right-wing heroine.

ROSA. Actually I was a Christian socialist. One more extinct species of the left. *(Low.)* Along with Social Workers who care too much. *(Bright.)* Right, what are we going to do? Do you go with a lawyer to this Sedgrove Enquiry?

ALICE. Oh listen to her! Come to put all to rights, and chased to London by evil Stasi man, wow!

ROSA. You will stop whirling around, you will pull yourself together.

ALICE. Whoops, will I?

ROSA *(looking at the crucifix. To herself)*. Could He have been called back for this? Joachim used to say, in the old days, He sends us to where we must be, whether we know it or not.

ALICE. There! You've gone religious on me! I knew you would, in the end. Oh no, big sister wouldn't let a chance like this go, without dumping Jesus on me. (ALICE *retches into the bowl. She can bring nothing up. She lies back. A weak smile. Then she clutches* ROSA's *wrist.*) I believed I understood her.

ROSA. Who? (*She hesitates.*) The baby's mother . . .?

ALICE. Cathay Pacific. Demetra dreamt of flying with Sylvester, on Cathay Pacific airlines.

ROSA. Flying where?

ALICE. Nowhere. Just flying over the Ocean. It was the only thing she ever told me, that she wanted . . . (*She is still gripping* ROSA's *wrist.*)

ROSA. It was 'unprofessional to empathise . . .'. But you did.

ALICE. Sometimes I think I've got her face . . .

ROSA (*frightened*). Alice . . .

ALICE. See, I knew that she'd gone back to Sylvester. I knew, I. I wanted them to . . . I don't know, or. Get it together, get on a FUCKING AEROPLANE, fly over the Pacific Ocean in the end, I . . .

She pulls ALICE *to her. They embrace.* ALICE *leans her head on* ROSA's *shoulder.*

ROSA. It's alright, it's alright. (*Stroking* ALICE's *hair.*) What could be more despicable than you and I? We wanted to put the world to rights. We were the high achievers, we were the technicians for DOING GOOD, we were the 'change the worlders'. But we're despicable, we're the lowest of the low, because we failed . . . So what shall we do? Make a penance? Go and eat earth? In a London park? Boil STONES for supper?

ALICE. Oh yeah? Be nuns and whip ourselves. And shine.

ROSA. Upwardly?

ALICE. Upwardly.

ROSA. We could plead medical difficulties, with the Enquiry. There is a clinic, in Baden-Baden, in West Germany, I do have

SOME professional contacts, we could get you . . .

ALICE *pulls away from her angrily.*

Enter SANDY. *He carries a six pack of lager cans. At the same time* ROSA *goes to the corner of the room and retrieves the file.*

ALICE. Why aren't you on guard duty? Go on! Woof woof.

SANDY. Nah, give us a break, it's getting cold out there again, I mean it was fucking HAILING this morning. Not fucking NATURAL is it, hailing at fucking Easter. *(He hesitates.)* Look, er, want a beer?

ALICE *holds out a hand. He throws her a can. She catches it, opens it and drinks.*

ALICE. Happy Sandy?

SANDY. You what?

ALICE *(to* ROSA). You know, I'm afraid that you and I are torturing ourselves, smashing our lives up, over . . . over a world that most of the GREAT THEM, like our SANDY here, don't even know exists.

ROSA. Alice that's not the point . . .

ALICE. Oh it is the point . . .

SANDY. IGNORANT. She hangs on to that with both hands, does our Alice, me being fucking IGNORANT. I tell you clever-clever cows, I know what I fucking need to know and I fucking get by on it. Can you two say that? Do you know what you need to know? Do you get by on it? The fuck do you. I mean look at you, eh? Eh?

ROSA. No, Sandy. I don't know what I need to know.

SANDY. Well then! *(He struggles with himself. Then tears a can from the six-pack.)* Have a can of lager then.

He lobs a can at ROSA *who is surprised to find herself catch it. He sits down opening a can himself.* ALICE *giggles at him. The three with lager cans in their hands. Suddenly they all look in unison at* JOANNE *in her headstand.*

And –

2.

'BERTIE' *pushes open the door and enters. They look at him in unison.*
NB: 'BERTIE' *reverts to the slight accent of Act One.*

'BERTIE'. Good evening. Is it usual to have hail in England, at
Easter time?

At once change.

Aside No. 4. 'The House in the Forest'

'BERTIE'

Dear little house I built
          deep
In the forests of our Germany

Dear path
          secret beneath the trees
To the hallowed hearth

Where heart
          took its ease
And mind cleaned its pain

And smoke of woodfire
          hung in leaves after rain

And water's lap
          crystal on stones in stream

Brought rest
          to conscience
Brought peace to dreams –

And great nights drinking!
          With owls calling
Elves and lost souls calling

I and my guests out
          to pissed-out of the mind
dancing, stark naked in a clearing

By blazing
          fire, wine
Running down mouth to arms to legs

Oh to be deeply drunk again
          deep
In the forests of our Germany

But –

A pause.

Have they sold you, yet
         dear little house I built
Dear secret policeman's perk?

Have they sold you to a Jap
         or a jerk
Of an American

Or a Bonn politician
         for the hunting
Playing at Hermann Goering

Or a Moscow
         Mafioso Chief
Who needs a safe retreat

From police
         on to loads
Of unsafe Polish meat

Or a banking adviser
         a wanking Englishman
With mobile telephone

Or –

Are you
         alone
Rotting

Your wooden walls
         returning
To the loam

The dark, rich loam
         of ancient Prussia
Our German mother –

Hold hard, little house
         hold bolts to the roof beams
Keep high the lintel of your door

I will be back
         I will light
Your hearth again

I will know peace

Once more, deep
In the forests of our Germany.

Change: the scene is restored. 'BERTIE', exactly as before.

'BERTIE'. Good evening. Is it usual to have hail in England, at
Easter time?

ROSA, *staring at the file which lies in full view on the carpet.* SANDY
stands. He circles 'BERTIE'. *In this scene* 'BERTIE' *has a newly
assumed mild manner. It comes and goes unpredictably.*

(To ALICE.) You must forgive the intrusion.

ALICE. Must I?

'BERTIE'. Yes the English weather. I should . . . ah . . . buy a
'brolley'? As a souvenir? *(He pauses.)* Rosa, please do not . . .
(He sighs.) Do not be distressed at my seeking you out. It is not
what you may fear. You have no reason for any upset.
(Indicating JOANNE *in her handstand.)* Your young friend has
gifts.

ROSA *(low)*. What are you doing here?

'BERTIE'. I am in London for business, business. Ach, the suit, I
know. GDR tailoring. Perhaps I should sell it, second-hand? In
your Portobello Road? It may create a strange fashion.

ROSA *and* ALICE *are dead still.*

But, slowly, we 'EASTIES' take the first, faltering steps, as
traders upon strange shores. It is difficult. We are both too
trusting and too suspicious.

ROSA. How did you even find me here?

'BERTIE' *(shrugs)*. Oh, nothing too serious. Your sister used to
write to you? Her address was on her letters? I have made a
few notes, from the old days you know, of things that may be to
hand. Be 'handy'.

ALICE *(low)*. Jesus Christ . . .

'BERTIE'. PLEASE do not be alarmed. And since I am here on
business . . .

ROSA. You're lying. There's no 'business'. I know what you've
come to London for.

'BERTIE'. Oh yes?

ROSA. 'The dog to its vomit'.

'BERTIE'. I am charmed.

Behind 'BERTIE'*s back,* SANDY *picks up the lump of plaster of Paris.*

ALICE. Just get out. My sister doesn't want to talk to you.

'BERTIE'. I suspect she does.

SANDY *crashes the lump of plaster of Paris down on* 'BERTIE'*s head. It splinters and powders. It has no effect on* 'BERTIE' *at all. He turns and looks at* SANDY. *A silence.*

SANDY. Sorry.

'BERTIE' *(puts his raincoat and briefcase down slowly. With deliberation he flicks a hand at his lapels. He smiles. He indicates* JOANNE *who has not flinched in her headstand).* The untouchable calm of the Orient, if only we had that in Europe. The self-control to allow the mind to float upon nothingness, the beautiful absurdity of the Zen archer, blind-folded, whose arrow always hits the bullseye.

And he turns with one quick movement and slams his knuckles into SANDY'*s solar plexus.* SANDY *is so winded by the blow that he cannot cry out. He sinks to the floor and doubles over clutching his midriff.* ROSA *and* ALICE *are too frightened to move.*

ROSA. That's it there.

'BERTIE', *uncomprehending.*

ROSA. What you came for, there.

'BERTIE' *looks at the file.*

Take it and go.

A pause. Then 'BERTIE' *leans over the suffering* SANDY. *He runs his hand over his shoulders.*

'BERTIE' *(low).* Don't try too hard to breathe, take one deep breath, hold, breathe out. The muscles will relax, the pain will be better. *(A pat on* SANDY'*s back.)*

SANDY. Uh.

'BERTIE'. Bah! The old skills are redundant, I know. Karate blows are of little use when negotiating a hard-currency loan with the manager of the Kensington High Street Branch of your

Barclay's Bank. But I am seeking retraining! *(He points at the file.)* What is that?

ROSA *(pauses)*. Your 'good faith'.

'BERTIE'. You lose me . . .

ROSA. The names you gave me in Berlin.

'BERTIE'. Oh? *(He realises. He smiles.)* Oh.

ALICE. It's what?

ROSA. It's a list of collaborators with the old regime. You read down a column of names. They are meaningless. Then suddenly you see a name, and you see a face that you know, the look in an eye that you know, a voice . . .

ALICE. You mean . . . Joachim is on the list?

SANDY *(croaking)*. List?

ALICE *(angrily at him, continuing to look at ROSA)*. It's a list of agents of the Stasi.

SANDY. A list of fucking Nazis?

ALICE. Not NAZIS. The STASI. Of the old communist regime in East Germany.

SANDY. You what?

ALICE *(furious at him)*. Of the other half of Germany, what is in two halves . . .

SANDY. I know that! *(A moment.)* Do I?

ROSA. For Godsake! Joachim's name is on the list.

A pause.

ALICE. I don't believe that. The blue eyes, the childlike look? No. That can't be right.

ROSA *(to ALICE)*. Why not? Feet of clay? Who wasn't contaminated? Who didn't, once, deal with them, do something, someone down the years, of which they were ashamed?

ALICE. You've left the good Saint Joachim?

'BERTIE' *smiles.*

ROSA. I was a foreigner. I could always leave. Come back home to my 'exemplary sister'.

'BERTIE'. I did give you that file. To do so was irresistible. But
. . . unpleasant.

ALICE. 'UNPLEASANT?' It's destroyed her marriage. *(To
ROSA.)* Burn the fucking thing.

'BERTIE' *(to ALICE)*. Tch tkh, difficult. It is history, you see.

ALICE. Burn it. Burn ALL the files.

'BERTIE'. Myself, Miss Alice, I have no problem with that. But
there are moralists among us who do. There is a proposal that
the Ministry of State Security files be buried, under a green
mound in the centre of Berlin. Like Hitler's bunker? The
mound will be a monument to the abnormal normality of our
era, yes? As the Führer bunker was a monument to another . . .
massive abnormal normality. AND when we are all dead, the
archaeologists of the future can dig up the truth about us all.

ALICE. Then . . . publish the lot. Joachim and all the bastards.

'BERTIE' *(gently)*. My dear, society would fall to pieces. How can
an entire nation of collaborators, gaol itself? *(Eyeing her.)* I
mean, who leads an exemplary life? Do you?

ALICE *(suddenly frightened)*. You don't know anything about me.
How can you know anything about me?

ROSA. You've come here for the list, because your new friends
are on it. It'll destroy you.

'BERTIE'. No no, we are all now 'reborn anew', I and my
comrades. I am a Dutchman, with passport to prove it. I am
even learning Dutch. A boring language, excellent for the
bourgeois gentilhomme I seek to become. And I'm thinking of
becoming very fat . . . *(Laughs.)* The fat do well in business.
(Leaning over ALICE's shoulder.) In Amsterdam, I see something
of drugs. Is that your problem?

ALICE, *dead still.*

ROSA. Don't go near her, leave her alone! You gave me the file of
names in a fit of conscience. Now you bitterly regret it.

'BERTIE' *(he sighs)*. No, that is not why I am here. *(A pause.)* I
am here for you, Rosa. Come away with me, marry me.

*A horrible silence, all still. 'BERTIE' is smiling. JOANNE comes out
of her headstand and looks at 'BERTIE'.*

We are two of a kind. Both of us born into great faiths? My

father was an underground communist party member in the Nazi time, one of the heroic generation. I was the privileged son of a hero in the struggle against fascism. I had great power. As a 'Stasiman', I could fuck anyone I passed in the street, anyone.

SANDY *steps toward* 'BERTIE' *who turns and looks at him disparagingly.* SANDY *stops in his tracks.*

(*To* ROSA.) Yes, are one of a kind. We have both been scoured clean. I of socialism, you of Jesus.

ROSA. It's strange. When you're a Christian, or have been a Christian, all kinds of people come up to you and think they can talk to you about Jesus. Religion's like the weather, everyone's an expert on it . . .

'BERTIE'. No no, Rosa. When I came to see you in Berlin I could sense your faith leaving you. Like a sweetness, sweating out of you. I still smell it, it has clung to me.

ALICE. Don't speak to this joker, have nothing to do with him.

ROSA (*to* ALICE). No it's alright. (*To* BERTIE.) It's strange. That night in the East, you seemed so formidable. Dangerous and terrible. But standing here in London, just a few months on . . . you look . . . diminished. Grubby. Nothing at all. (*Angrily.*) You talk of faiths, and losing faiths . . . You have no idea what it is like. No idea at all. To suddenly see Creation . . . not as from God's hand, but as an horrific kind of . . . entity. A huge amoeba . . . of meaningless life, with its slime everywhere, on everything, on your thoughts, even on things, your clothes, the food you eat . . . you cannot possibly have any idea of the disgust.

'BERTIE'. Then let us reconstruct ourselves.

ALICE. What the hell do you mean? As a make-believe Dutch couple, with a little house by a canal, waddling about with clogs on?

'BERTIE' (*turning on* ALICE, *viciously*). You are from the West. You can have no idea of what is between your sister and I. The terrible intimacy that has bound us together. (*To* ROSA.) Let us slough off these skins. Marry me. (*A smiling glance at* ALICE.) And yes, we will be Dutch, the Dutch are an excellent race, they invented modern capitalism in their damp little country. And still they are merchants, Dutchmen sell anything all over the world, diamonds, guns, most amenable people. *(Low to* ROSA.) I have thought about you. You have . . . *(Hesitates.)* Inside me. I am sincere.

ALICE. Swat him down, Rosa. Tread on him.

A silence. ROSA *and* 'BERTIE' *looking at each other. Then he turns away with a sigh.*

'BERTIE'. But then, on the other hand, perhaps I am not. *(He picks up his briefcase.)* I assure you, I had forgotten about these wretched, useless pages. *(A pause.)* You must have been aware at once, of their worthlessness? *(The old hard edge in his voice.)* Yes yes. We doctored the files. 'Disinformation'! It was a major operation, underway all that summer. Fake payments to innocents, forged reports from innocents . . . jumbled up with the real 'Judases'. One cannot be told from the other. *(A grin.)* Look on it as a vast practical joke. *(To* SANDY.) Do not worry I am recovering.

ROSA. A vast practical joke.

'BERTIE'. There will be no clean . . . *(A gesture with his hand.)* . . . guillotining of the past, Rosa. All will be muddle and evasion. The new 'democratic' Germany is contaminated before it has even begun. *(He picks up the file and offers it to* ROSA.) Keep it. It is a curio. With lumps of the wall, old Hero of Labour medals, old Stasi uniforms?

ROSA *takes the file, shakily.*

(He smiles.) I can see there is little chance of you continuing my therapy, so expertly begun in Berlin . . .

ALICE. Go. Just go.

'BERTIE'. One moment, if you will forgive me, there may be a little matter of business here. One must spot the chance to make money, that is a secret of the free market. *(To* SANDY.) Are you employed, my friend?

ALICE. What?

'BERTIE' *sets his briefcase on the carpet and crouches on his haunches before it. He takes out a small black machine.* ROSA, JOANNE *and* ALICE *look at it.* SANDY *reacts with great interest.*

SANDY. Here! That a Sega Megadrive?

'BERTIE'. Sixteen bit.

SANDY. Fucking ace.

'BERTIE'. You are familiar with the Megadrive?

SANDY. Flogged games for it, didn't I, for this face down East Street market. But they was all in fucking Japanese and anyway they didn't fucking work.

'BERTIE'. Ah yes, the Japanese seek to make the games unworkable, on illegally exported machines.

SANDY. Yeah, I had fucking mums complaining all over me, 'cos little Johnnie's new game was fucked, it was all very dodgy, then the face that was running the stall did a bunk.

'BERTIE'. These machines are fully adapted to Western television systems.

SANDY. PAL adapted, yeah? How you manage that?

'BERTIE'. There is a little workshop in Kentish Town. With Berlin connections.

SANDY. You into PC engines?

'BERTIE'. You favour the PC engine?

SANDY. Fucking brilliant little thing, in't it. Eight bit chip but comes on like a sixteen bit.

'BERTIE'. But you need a CD Rom attachment, at three hundred pounds each? And in the final analysis, it is only eight bit.

SANDY. What do you think of the New World Neo Geo from SKN? Load of fucking rubbish?

'BERTIE'. Brilliant, arcade quality, a sixty-four megabyte machine, with machismo . . .

SANDY. Got a joy stick too . . .

'BERTIE'. Mm . . . but the games are too expensive, and have infinite continues. The kids don't like that. It will fail in the market. The Megadrive is king.

ROSA (to ALICE). What are they talking about?

ALICE (to ROSA). Video game machines.

ROSA. Oh.

'BERTIE' *takes out three video game cassettes and hands them to* SANDY, *who takes them eagerly.*

'BERTIE'. These you know?

SANDY. 'Super Shinobi'. That's the Ninja one in't it. 'Golden Axe.' 'Ghouls and Ghosts' . . . these are right up there, these are the fucking top . . .

ROSA *(to* 'BERTIE'). What are you doing? What is this?

'BERTIE' *(to* SANDY). State of the art. You don't . . . notice anything about them?

SANDY. Should I? *(He looks at the cassettes.)* You mean they're bent?

'BERTIE'. Cheap copies, illegally produced. *(He smiles at* ROSA.)

SANDY. Yeah but . . . you can't copy video games, the fucking Japs build blocks in the fucking programming, uncrackable . . .

'BERTIE' *(still smiling at* ROSA). Oh anything can be 'cracked'. Some ex-colleagues of mine in Berlin are highly skilled. We make the copies of the games in Warsaw. Conditions in Poland are excellent. AND . . . now we have Kentish Town. *(A pause – and he is still looking at* ROSA.) The East opens like a flower after rain? Populations starved of fantasy . . . Western television sets are selling everywhere, to sell video machines and games to play on them . . . it is as easy as giving sweets away, in a time of famine.

ROSA *closes her eyes.*

(To SANDY.) So there are street markets in London, where video games are sold?

SANDY. Games and machines are flogged all over. It's fucking cowboy-time out there.

'BERTIE'. As a native of this area, would you be a salesman for my company?

SANDY. Oh. Well . . .

'BERTIE'. Keep those.

SANDY. I haven't got a fucking Megadrive . . .

'BERTIE' *(handing the machine to* SANDY). Have it.

SANDY. What? No . . .

'BERTIE'. It's yours.

SANDY. Oh. *(Staring at the machine in his hands.)* Thank you very much.

'BERTIE'. Your public house is the institution on Camberwell Green?

SANDY. The 'Hermits Cave', yeah . . .

'BERTIE'. So let's have a beer.

SANDY. Right!

'BERTIE'. We will discuss arrangements. We must be . . . *(A finger to his lips.)* . . . stumm.

SANDY. Oh, yeah, course, mum's the word if this is fucking bent. Got a bag for these Alice? Fucking carrier in here . . .

ALICE does not look at him. SANDY finds a carrier bag and puts the games and the machine in it. He stands by the door eager to go.

'BERTIE', snapping his briefcase shut.

'BERTIE' *(to* ROSA). There is a video game. It's German. The game is called 'Aryan Test'. Players become concentration camp managers, they have to spot who is a Jew who is not, prevent mass escape etcetera. The game contravenes laws forbidding the propagation of hatred, but the police cannot track down its makers. *(He smiles.)* By next Easter, I could be a millionaire. A materialist salvation at least, Rosa.

He bends over JOANNE and begins to whisper to her. She comes out of her headstand. She looks up at him, startled.

ROSA. Are you going to tell me?

'BERTIE' is still, his lips at JOANNE's ear.

Did you put my husband's name on the list?

'BERTIE' whispering to JOANNE.

Was that 'disinformation'?

JOANNE shakes her head sharply.

ALICE. Leave her alone!

'BERTIE' still whispers to JOANNE.

Get your filthy mouth away from her!

He gives JOANNE a card from his pocket. He straightens and looks at them.

ROSA. Was Joachim really on the list? *(A pause.)* Or did you fake it? *(A pause.)* As part of the joke? *(A pause.)* You must tell me. Clearly you must see, why you must tell me.

'BERTIE' *smiles and exits.*

SANDY. What a great bloke. There's fucking dosh there, I can smell it. We'll really do this place up, it'll be chunky armchairs, fucking flock wallpaper 'fore you know it, eh, Alice? Splash out on a bit of fucking LIVING. *(He hesitates for a moment.)* I'll just nip out for a beer with Bertie then. *(He exits.)*

A silence.

ALICE *(to JOANNE).* What did he say to you?

ROSA *(to herself).* I trusted the list and not Joachim.

JOANNE *(to ALICE).* Nothing.

ALICE *(to JOANNE).* What did he give you? Show it to me.

ROSA *(to herself).* I trusted a bit of paper, not the man. Now the bit of paper itself, can't be trusted.

JOANNE *hands* ALICE *the card.* ALICE *looks at it, frowns and hands it to* ROSA.

What is it?

ROSA *(she looks at it).* It's the address of The Chameleon Club. It's a Berlin night spot.

ALICE. His lair, his base . . .

ROSA. It's cabaret for mime in West Berlin, it's well known. He was recommending it to her, that's all. *(To herself.)* I stepped out of my marriage, I stepped out of everything I believe in. *(She turns away.)*

JOANNE. Maybe I'll go there.

ALICE. You what?

JOANNE *(shrugs).* Maybe I can get a gig there. I can do my hanged man.

ALICE. Have nothing to do with him.

JOANNE. If it's a gig it's a gig.

ALICE. For godsake, he'll say 'meet me in Berlin' to every little girl along the way. Have nothing AT ALL to do with that man.

Look what he's done to Rosa.

ROSA *(she turns back)*. At first, it was Joachim's fault. I became unable to stand it, when he talked to the people we were helping. I heard false notes in his voice when he prayed with them , insincere ... I began to think, 'is God with us?' We had terrible rows! I accused Joachim of having no faith, when all the time it was I, I who was becoming faithless to the Lord.

ALICE. Alright! Sister!

ROSA. No! *(A pause.)* No. *(A pause.)* When I saw Joachim on the list, it was so simple to make the leap! 'The priest is false and so is his God.' I nearly went mad, I was obscene in my mind, I imagined doing terrible things, even with Jesus. Then that went. And now, the world isn't repulsive anymore ... it's flat.

ALICE. You still brought THAT ... *(Points at the crucifix.)* with you.

ROSA. The form not the content, the language not the meaning ... *(Low)*. Alice, I don't know how I'll do the simplest things from now on, even ... how I'll raise my hand to my face. *(She turns her hand and looks at it.)*

ALICE. I don't know how, go through these days, have any future at all, how CAN I know?

JOANNE *(interrupting)*. WHY ... *(She is angry. She forces questions from herself.)*

WHY don't we get the ferry?

ALICE. What?

JOANNE *(difficulty)*. WHY ... Not? The ferry. Tomorrow midday. Southend to Rotterdam. That's how me and Dutch John was going to do it. You don't have to get a cabin. Rotterdam, then hitch to Amsterdam, and there're squats all over. Then get the routine together, and a week busking outside Central Station, and build up some dosh.

They stare at her.

(To ALICE.) That's how to do it.

ALICE. What are you talking about? *(She realises.)* Some kind of busking trip, what, to the South of France? To the magic city of Avignon? That's ridiculous.

JOANNE *(deflated)*. Yeah. WH ... No it's not ridiculous ... *(A pause.)* Not if we got the right mime.

ALICE. 'The bomb'?

JOANNE. No, you said the bomb was shit. *(She pauses.)* I got another routine. For you, me and her.

ALICE. Oh. Wonderful. right, what have we here? We've a religious nutcase who's lost Jesus, we've a drugged-up suspended social worker with a dead baby in her head, we've a runaway who does mime with probably several masked veneral infections . . .

ROSA starts at that and looks at JOANNE.

. . . who does mime and goes begging in the street . . . We are great stuff girls, we are great potential, we are a terrific cocktail. *(To JOANNE.)* Ridiculous, ridiculous. Has your generation NOTHING serious to offer the HUMAN WEAL at all?

JOANNE is angry.

JOANNE *(to ALICE).* With you, WHY tear yourself to bits 'cos a monster's done something terrible to a baby? *(To ROSA.)* With you, why let that Berlin bastard into your head? WHY say a thing's dead 'cos HE wants it dead?

ALICE. I don't need some guru-ed, diseased little tramp off the street to tell me . . . *(She stops.)*

She controls herself. A silence.

(To ROSA.) Would you do that? Run away?

ROSA *(to ALICE).* Would you?

ALICE *(irritated).* No, would YOU? Run away, from Joachim and Jesus?

ROSA. Would you run away from an official enquiry headed by a QC?

ALICE. Could you, or, just . . . leave your Berlin nightmare, and never think about it, ever again?

ROSA. Sister, could you, just run from what they're going to say about you in the newspapers?

ALICE *(to herself).* My picture next to the picture of a dead baby, 'Social worker blamed'.

ROSA. Leave the mess by the roadside, and never think about it again? Could you just disappear?

ALICE *(low)*. Yes, Could you?

ROSA *(low)*. Why do you think I came to London?

JOANNE *(interrupting)*. Got any cards?

ALICE. Any what?

JOANNE. Credit cards.

ALICE. The hole in the wall ate my Access weeks ago.

ROSA. Actually, I've got a Visa Gold Card.

At once, a change.

A dream of Good People

ALICE.

I want to find the door
              to the villages
It'll be an ordinary door
              in an ordinary wall
One day I'll come across it
              in a derelict house
A cellar
              a grafitti'd garage door
On a run-down estate
              and through I'll go –
Into that landscape
              And there they will be
Turning toward me
              the villagers
Difficult people
              to catch
The light must be right
              even to glimpse them –
Difficult people to know
              dangerous to us
for
              How shocking it would be
To meet
              a human being who

Has
        no
                fear –
A woman
        coming toward me.

   A pause.

And she'll give me
        a jewel –
Small, not
        glass, not stone not metal
Not
        polished wood –
Shining
        now-you-see-it
Now-you-don't –
        and of a colour
That's new
        And then she'll vanish
And I'll wake up
        back in the old armpit
Of a South London morning –

But
        there it'll be
The jewel
        she gave me.

   Change: the scene is restored.

ROSA. Actually, I've got a Visa Gold Card.

ALICE. You . . . have got . . . a Gold Card?

ROSA. I arranged it in West Berlin, ten years ago. Just in case Joachim and I ever needed money quickly. I've never used it.

JOANNE. Great! We'll get the midday boat. And when we're on the road you'll be amazed at the dosh. Three women, it's a good gimmick.

ROSA *(to ALICE)*. Are we going to do this, sister mine?

ALICE. Oh yes. *(Sing-song.)* . . . We the Brine sisters, brought up to DO GOOD in the world, have, by believing so HARD in things, strewn human wreckage all around . . . If the Brine sisters stop *trying* for bloody sainthood, may be they'll achieve something by accident.

JOANNE. Right. Get in a line.

She pushes ROSA *and* ALICE *about.*

JOANNE. It's a flying trick, it'll be GREAT with three. We'll try it now.

ROSA. Eh . . .

ALICE. Eh . . .

JOANNE. Come on, don't moan about it. Hands round waists.

JOANNE *pulls* ROSA *and* JOANNE *into a line either side of her. They hold each other's waists.*

JOANNE. I saw a man be a human bomb once. Everyone in the crowd swore they saw him just EXPLODE in front of them. So we can do this. Come on.

ROSA. Try what? WHAT?

JOANNE. Flying nuns, that's the routine. I've worked it out, it's a great angle, we can do things with the skirts.

ALICE. The three flying nuns.

ROSA. Look, if we really are going to do this, maybe we should book ahead. I'd like to stay in a hotel, just now and then . . .

JOANNE. First step. Left foot . . . and down in front of right foot. One . . . two . . . three . . . and . . .

ALICE *loses balance and she and* ROSA *smirk.* JOANNE, *sternly.*

Do it properly!

ROSA. We're very sorry.

JOANNE. Get it right and they'll all swear they saw us fly. One . . . two . . . three . . . and . . .

They complete the step in unison.

And up.

They are rising on their toes as – a blackout.